A Bluestocking Guide

World War I

by

Jane A. Williams

based on Richard J. Maybury's book
WORLD WAR I

published by
Bluestocking Press

web site: www.BluestockingPress.com
Phone 800-959-8586

Printed and bound in the United States of America.
Cover illustration by Bob O'Hara, Georgetown, CA
Cover design by Brian C. Williams, El Dorado, CA
Edited by Jane A. Williams

ISBN-10: 0-942617-58-4
ISBN-13: 978-0-942617-58-0

Published by

Bluestocking Press • Post Office Box 1014
Placerville, CA 95667-1014 • Phone: 800-959-8586
web site: www.BluestockingPress.com

Contents

Bluestocking Guides are designed to reinforce and enhance a student's understanding of the subject presented in the primer. The subject for this study guide is the World Wars. The primer is WORLD WAR I by Richard J. Maybury.

Given the wide range of age and ability levels of individuals who read WORLD WAR I, it is suggested that students complete the exercises in this study guide that are most age-appropriate or ability-appropriate for them.

Assignment of Exercises

While all given questions and assignments are designed to enhance the student's understanding and retention of the subject matter presented in the primer, it is by no means mandatory that each student complete every exercise in this study guide. This study guide is designed for flexibility based on a student's age, as well as a student's interest in the material presented.

It is strongly suggested that each student complete the Comprehension Exercises, but instructors can preview and then select the Application Exercises, Films to View, and Suggested Books to Read that they wish the student to complete, based on: course time available, student's interest, and/or student's age (some films/books might not be age appropriate — the student might be too young, too old, or the content too advanced for a younger student). Also, depending on the age and interest level of a student, one student might spend weeks on a research assignment, whereas another student might spend a few hours or days.

Suggested Time Frame For Study

This study guide is organized to allow the instructor flexibility in designing the ideal course of study. Therefore, there is no "right" or "wrong" time frame for covering the material; the instructor should tailor the study of the primer and study guide to the student's unique school schedule, learning style, and age. For example, younger students may only complete comprehension exercises, whereas older students may complete additional application exercises, suggested readings, and films.

An easy-to-apply rule of thumb for determining length of study is to divide the number of chapters in a primer by the number of weeks the instructor plans to study the subject/book.

Ideally, the student should read a chapter from the primer and then immediately answer the corresponding questions in the study guide. Chapter length varies, so sometimes a student may be able to read more than one chapter and complete the corresponding questions/exercises in a day. Some instructors may choose to complete the primer in a few short weeks in which case multiple chapters per day will need to be covered. Others may plan to study the primer over an entire semester, so only a few chapters per week will be assigned. The key is to move quickly enough that the student is engaged with learning and also able to absorb all concepts fully. The student's performance on end-of-chapter Questions and Assignments should be a good indication of this.

The time frame for completing application exercises (Discussion/Essay/Assignment/Research) is also subject to the instructor's discretion. Most discussions can take place immediately after reading the chapter. However, students may need a day or two to complete an essay, and some assignments will take outside research requiring additional time. It is best for the instructor to preview the application exercises (Discussion/Essay/Assignment/Research) and assign the student a "due date" based upon the student's cognitive abilities and available course schedule.

Comprehension Exercises

Comprehension Exercises test the degree to which the student understands and retains the information presented in each chapter. In this study guide Comprehension Exercises include: 1) Define, 2) True/False, and 3) Short Answer/ Fill-In. Students are encouraged to answer all exercises in complete sentences. The information needed to complete these exercises can usually be found in the given chapter of the primer. Answers will be found in the answer section of this Study Guide.

Define

The student should define the given term based on Richard Maybury's definition provided in the given chapter or glossary (*not* a standard dictionary definition). This is essential. As Richard Maybury says, "Fuzzy language causes fuzzy thinking." For any discussion or explanation to be clearly understood, one must first understand the intended definition of words as used by the author. Confusion and disagreement can occur because the student does not understand the author's intended definition of a word. To reinforce this point, have a student look up the word "law" in an unabridged Webster's dictionary. The student should find a number of definitions following the word "law." Again, unless one agrees on the definition intended for the discussion or study at hand, misunderstanding or "fuzzy thinking" can result.

True/False

For True/False exercises, if the student believes the statement is correct, the student should simply write "True" as the answer. If the student believes the statement is *not* true, the student should write "False." If the student answers the question "False," the student should be sure to state why the statement is *not* true or rewrite the false statement to make it true. In the answer section of this study guide, statements that are "False" are so noted and have been rewritten to make them true.

Short Answer/Fill In

The student should answer Short Answer/ Fill In questions based upon knowledge gained from studying the given chapter. Unless the student is asked to use his/her own opinion or knowledge, the answer should be based upon Richard Maybury's statements. Generally, Short Answer/Fill In Questions are selected verbatim from the given chapter.

Application Exercises

With few exceptions, Application Exercises ask the student to apply the knowledge and ideas he/she has gained from a given chapter to "real world" situations. In many cases, these assignments are designed to help the student personalize the information just learned so that the student can better retain and apply the knowledge. In this study guide application exercises include: 1) Discussion, 2) Essay, 3) Assignment, and 4) For Further Research. In the majority of instances, answers to Application Exercises will vary based upon the student's own experiences. Application Exercises are designed to encourage informal discussions among students and instructors, and/or to stimulate students to critically evaluate the scenario. However, the instructor may ask the student to write answers (in essay format, outline, etc.) if a more formal/ structure approach is desired.

For Further Reading or To View

The books and films mentioned in For Further Reading and To View are designed to expand students' understanding of concepts presented in the related chapter. No written or verbal reports on the books/movies are usually required, however, students and instructors are encouraged to discuss the ideas presented. Thus, Suggestions for Further Reading/Viewing usually have no set answers and, therefore, may not appear in the "Answer" section. (The instructor may choose to assign a book/movie report of his/her own construction if he/she desires.)

How to Grade Assignments

Define, True/False, Short Answer/Fill-In

To determine the percentage of correct answers, divide the total number of correct answers by the total number of questions. If, for example, a chapter section has two Define questions, one True/False question, and seven Short Answer/Fill-In questions, and the student has answered correctly eight of these questions, the student will have answered 80% of the questions correctly.

8 ÷ 10 = .80 (or 80%)

Number of Correct Answers ÷ Number of Total Questions
= Percentage of Questions Answered Correctly

In "Grade" equivalents, percentage scores generally range as follows:

90 - 100%	= A
80 - 89.9%	= B
70 - 79.9%	= C
60 - 69.9%	= D
less than 60%	= F

In general, a student earning an "A" has demonstrated excellent understanding of the subject matter; a student earning a "B" has demonstrated good understanding of the subject matter; a student earning a "C" has demonstrated sufficient understanding of the subject matter; and a student earning a "D" or "F" would benefit from reviewing the subject matter to strengthen his/her understanding of the topic at hand.

In determining whether a student has provided a "right" or "wrong" answer to a question, the instructor should compare the student's answers with the answers provided in this guide. True/False, Fill-In, and Define questions/answers are straightforward. Short Answer questions/answers are also generally straightforward; on some longer answers the student's wording may vary slightly from the answer provided in this study guide, but the student should receive full credit if the *content* of his/her answer is correct. When in doubt, it is recommended that the instructor refer back to the chapter in the primary text to reference what the author said about the issue at hand.

"Answers Will Vary"

In the answer section of this study guide you will sometimes come across an answer that reads "answers will vary" for a given question. This generally means that the student is required to answer the question using his/her own knowledge, experience, or intuition. In these instances, the instructor should refer back to the chapter in the primary text to reference what the author said about the issue at hand compared to the student's answer; a "correct" answer should be thoughtful, complete, and on-topic.

Discussion/Essay/Assignment

These assignments are provided so that students can apply the concepts they learned in the given chapter to their own experiences, current events, or historical events — to make the concepts more meaningful. In most cases, it is extremely difficult to "grade" the completed assignments as "right" or "wrong." Instead, the instructor should provide guidance for these assignments. The completeness, thoughtfulness, enthusiasm, and meaning the student brings to the assignment will serve as an indication of the student's mastery of the assignment. If the instructor then wishes to assign a grade, he/she may elect to do so. Or, these assignments may be non-graded "extra credit," serving to boost the student's overall grade for the course.

Uncle Eric's Model of How the World Works

Short Answer/Fill-In/True or False

1. What is a model as defined by Uncle Eric?

2. According to Uncle Eric, why are models important?

3. Why is it important to sort incoming data?

4. Are models rigid? Should they ever change?

5. What are the two models Uncle Eric believes are most reliable, as well as crucially important for everyone to learn? Why does he believe this?

6. _____________ is the political philosophy that is no philosophy at all. It embraces the concept that those in power can do whatever appears necessary to achieve their goals.

Discussion/Essay/Assignment

7. Other than Uncle Eric's model, can you provide other examples of models?

8. What purpose does the book WORLD WAR I have relative to Uncle Eric's Model?

9. Listen to, or read, politicians' political speeches, news conferences, news releases, etc., and note if, or how often, the politicians use the phrase "we will do whatever is necessary" to execute a proposal, fix a problem, etc. Do you think it is ever okay to "do whatever is necessary" to resolve a problem? Explain your answer.

10. Look up several of the following words in a dictionary and read their definitions: fascism, liberty, economics, history, republic, and democracy. Does each word have more than one definition? Why?

11. If a word has more than one definition, why is it important that an author define his/her meaning of a word about which he/she is writing?

12. Richard Feynman, a Nobel prize winning physicist, once said it didn't matter what something was called, so long as one understood the characteristics that go into making up what that thing is. It doesn't matter if we call the bird identified as a Blue Jay, a "Blue Jay," so long as we understand that the living creature called by that name has the following characteristics: The bird's food consists primarily of nuts and small seeds as well as insects. They lay from three to six eggs that are blue, green, or yellow with spots of brown or gray. They live for about four years. Another example might be: You might have different names during your lifetime, but you are still the same person. When you are born your parents might name you William. As a child, you might be Billy, or you might

be given a nickname (i.e. Laura Ingalls Wilder from the LITTLE HOUSE™ books was called Half-pint by her Pa). As a teenager you might be Bill or Will, then, as an adult, you might use the more formal William. In all these cases, with all these names, you are still you. If you are female, you might have a maiden name and a married name. Do you agree or disagree with Richard Feynman? Does it matter what something is called, so long as one understands the characteristics of the thing? Explain and provide support for your position.

For Further Reading

13. Read CAPITALISM FOR KIDS by Karl Hess for additional information on different political philosophies, particularly the chapter called "Capitalism and Other Isms." Published by Bluestocking Press, web site: www.BluestockingPress.com; Phone: 800-959-8586.

Author's Disclosure

Short Answer/Fill-In/True or False

1. What is Juris Naturalism?

Discussion/Essay/Assignment

2. In the "Author's Disclosure," Richard Maybury says that few writers disclose the viewpoints or opinions they use to decide what information is important and what is not, or what data will be presented and what data omitted. Collect several history books from your home library, school library, or public library. Do the authors of the books you collected disclose their viewpoints or opinions to the reader? Do the authors disclose what criteria they used to determine what information or data to include in the book and what to omit? Explain why it is, or is not, important to have biases disclosed. What benefit, if any, does a reader or viewer have (in the case of movies, televised news, or documentaries) if he/she is able to determine the viewpoint of a writer?

3. Uncle Eric says all history is slanted based on the facts historians choose to report. Can you provide examples of material you have read or to which you have listened where facts have been reported but perhaps not all the facts? If no books come to mind, have you had arguments or disagreements between siblings or friends in which, when asked, each person presented his/her side of the argument—presenting only those facts that best favored his/her side of the story? How can you learn to identify the slants of writers, news commentators, friends, etc.?

4. Read the quotes in the "Author's Disclosure" section of this book that help to describe the Juris Naturalist viewpoint. Look up the definition of "unalienable" in a current dictionary. Compare a current dictionary's definition with the definition from NOAH WEBSTER'S 1828 DICTIONARY: "Unalienable; that cannot be legally or justly alienated or transferred to another ... All men have certain natural rights which are inalienable."

5. Samuel Adams defined the natural rights of the colonists as the right to life, liberty, and property. Why do you think "property" was changed to "happiness" in the Declaration of Independence? *(Optional exercise: You can turn this into a research exercise by researching primary source documents of America's Founders to see if you can find the answer for the change from "property" to "happiness." Provide support for your position.)*

6. Select one of the quotes from the "Author's Disclosure" section of this book and write a short essay about what the quote means to you.

For Further Reading

7. Read HOW TO LIE WITH STATISTICS by Darrell Huff, published by W.W. Norton, and distributed by Bluestocking Press, web site: www.BluestockingPress.com; Phone: 800-959-8586. Excellent book. A modern classic. Shows how statistics can distort truth. For ages 14 and up.

8. Read EVALUATING BOOKS: WHAT WOULD THOMAS JEFFERSON THINK ABOUT THIS? an Uncle Eric book by Richard J. Maybury. This book provides key indicators and terms to help the reader learn how to identify the slants of authors, media commentators, and others. Published by Bluestocking Press, web site: www.BluestockingPress.com; Phone: 800-959-8586. For ages 12 and up.

9. Visit www.worldpress.org on the Internet. Many articles posted on this site list the author and his/her philosophical viewpoint, i.e., Centrist, Libertarian, Liberal, Conservative. Have someone cover up the name and philosophical identity of each author and then read the articles. Can you identify each author's philosophical viewpoint? For help with this exercise, if a student has limited knowledge of political and economic biases, the student should first read Richard J. Maybury's books: EVALUATING BOOKS: WHAT WOULD THOMAS JEFFERSON THINK ABOUT THIS? and ARE YOU LIBERAL? CONSERVATIVE? OR CONFUSED? published by Bluestocking Press.

Note

Web sites change often but, at the time of publication, the following web site provides hundreds of World War links, so it's a good first place to begin research.
http://www.killeenroos.com/link/war.htm

Thought Exercises

Before you begin to read WORLD WAR I, answer the following questions. Your answers should be based on your current knowledge and/or opinions. (If you have no knowledge of the issue/topic, say so.) Save your responses. You will revisit these questions at a later time. After you have answered the questions, you may begin to read WORLD WAR I.

1. Write an essay on what patriotism means to you. Provide three examples from history in which individuals demonstrated through their actions your definition of patriotism.

2. Based on your current knowledge and opinions, write an essay detailing what caused World War I and World War II, what countries were on what side, who won, what were the results of the wars, etc.

3. What is the difference, if any, between international "neutrality" and "isolationism"?

Application Exercise

Before you begin to read this book, select a country that is currently engaged in armed conflict. As you read this book, apply what you learn to events that have caused the armed conflict, as well as to events that may continue to unfold. Keep a portfolio that will contain your research, opinions, ideas, and conclusions.

For example, what caused the country to become engaged in armed conflict? What alliances, if any, has that country formed? Have any abuses of political power occurred within that country? If so, by whom, and in what way? What are the economic and legal principles on which the country is based? What type of government does the country have?

Pay attention to the words and phrases that might be used in political speeches regarding the armed conflict. Watch for emotionally charged words versus those that appeal to reason. Read media stories that cover the conflict (on the Internet, international stories can be found at www.worldpress.org).

By the time you finish reading Richard Maybury's WORLD WAR I, determine what your position is regarding the merits of the armed conflict and write an essay explaining your position. Your "Country in Armed Conflict" portfolio should be completed and given to your instructor prior to taking the final exam.

Dedication

1. The dedication in this book reads: "To the independent thinkers who refuse to march off to war until they fully understand the opponent's point of view, and only after they have seen a mountain of evidence that the war is for an extremely good reason." Explain why you agree or disagree with this statement. If you disagree, under what circumstances do you think a soldier should blindly march off to war?

Cast of Characters

1. Complete one of the following activities:

    a. Write a biographical essay based on one of the individuals listed in the Cast of Characters.

    b. Write a one-act biographical play based on the life of an individual listed in the Cast of Characters. If you're really ambitious, perform it as well.

2. No women are listed in the Cast of Characters. Why?

3. On a piece of paper, make four columns. Title the columns as follows:

    Allies—World War I *Allies—World War II*

    Central Powers—World War I *Axis—World War II*

    Place the countries that formed each group under the appropriate heading.

The CARS Checklist for Research Source Evaluation

Credibility • **A**ccuracy • **R**easonableness • **S**upport

The CARS checklist is designed to provide criteria for evaluating the quality and reliability of a source. By applying the CARS checklist you will be better able to separate high-quality from poor quality information to any research you conduct. You will be better prepared to critically evaluate data and expert opinions, which will better equip you to excel in school, career, and life. Read more about the CARS checklist for Research Source Evaluation at one or more of the Internet sites below. (If these sites are no longer available, then conduct an Internet search for "CARS checklist" and click on a university/college link to an explanatory article.)

http://www.virtualsalt.com/evalu8it.htm
www.ru.ac.za/library/infolit/cars.html
http://www.mhhe.com/socscience/english/allwrite3/seyler/ssite/seyler/se03/cars.mhtml

Chapter 1: The 58-Year Persecution

Define

1. Patriotism:

2. Economics:

Short Answer/Fill-In/True or False

3. When Chris asks Uncle Eric to talk about WWII, why does Uncle Eric choose to begin with events leading to WWI?

4. What does Uncle Eric believe is the greatest weakness in education today?

5. Name the two laws that make civilization possible.

6. Which of the two laws is the basis of contract law?

7. Which of the two laws is the basis of tort law and some criminal law?

8. What is Uncle Eric's approach to writing about the World Wars?

9. What is Uncle Eric's purpose in writing this series of letters about the World Wars?

10. On whose principles are Uncle Eric's conclusions and observations based? What are these principles?

11. What did America's Founders believe about political power?

12. What subject does Uncle Eric say he will delve deeply into and that is rarely touched upon in other history books?

13. Uncle Eric says, "The government and the country are not the same thing." Explain why you agree or disagree with this statement.

14. According to Uncle Eric, the blame for World War II has shifted from what group to what other group?

15. Ralph Waldo Emerson said: "When a whole nation is roaring Patriotism at the top of its voice, I am fain to explore the cleanness of its hands and purity of its heart." Can you give examples from recent U.S. history "when a whole nation is roaring Patriotism at the top of its voice"?

For Research and Discussion

16. Mark Twain said, "My kind of loyalty was loyalty to one's country, not to its institutions or its office holders." Provide examples from U.S. or world history in which individuals or a group demonstrated through their actions that they chose country over their country's institutions or its officeholders.

17. Uncle Eric says that governments violate the two laws endlessly and each violation helps set the stage for new disasters, which then become the excuse for more violations. Give examples of governments violating these two laws. First list the law, then the example that violated the law.

18. Uncle Eric says, "In actual practice, my country right or wrong means my government right or wrong. This definition of patriotism leads to doing whatever the government says, even if it is not ethical." Can you give examples from world and U.S. history in which the government acted in unethical ways?

19. Uncle Eric says: "Kimmel and Short are generally blamed for the disaster at Pearl Harbor. Americans have been taught that these men had been warned to be ready for an attack, but neglected to prepare, and their forces were caught by surprise." What do other history books say about this incident?

20. Check your history books and determine how often, if at all, the author discusses economic connections when discussing historical events.

Chapter 2: The Grim Statistics

Short Answer/Fill-In/True or False

1. The ______________ government switched sides in World War I, starting the war on the side of the Central Powers and ending on the side of the Allies.

Assignment

2. Per the suggestion in this chapter, locate each country on a globe or world map. Use the same colored marker to identify the nations that comprised the Allied Powers and a different colored marker to identify the nations that comprised the Central Powers.

Chapter 3: Is Now the Time to Learn About War?

Define

1. Statist:

2. Nonstatist

For Research and Discussion

3. Uncle Eric tells Chris to look at old World War I and World War II recruitment posters. Check your local library for books with old recruitment posters. Dover Publications publishes: WORLD WAR II POSTERS and WORLD WAR I POSTERS. What emotions are the posters appealing to? In your opinion, explain why those same posters would, or would not be, successful today.

   Sources of World War I Posters on the Internet
   http://www.library.georgetown.edu/dept/speccoll/amposter.htm

   http://www.worldwar1.com/posters.htm

   http://afsf.lackland.af.mil/Images/WWI/

   Sources of World War II Posters on the Internet
   http://www.archives.gov/exhibit_hall/powers_of_persuasion/powers_of_persuasion_intro.html

   http://www.trumanlibrary.org/museum/posters/

   http://www.library.northwestern.edu/govpub/collections/wwii-posters/

4. During peacetime in America, what slogans have been used to encourage young men and women to enlist in the military? Explain how these advertising/marketing efforts appeal to you—or fail to appeal to you.

Chapter 4: First Ideas, Then Battles

Define

1. Diplomacy:

2. Geopolitical:

Short Answer/Fill-In/True or False

3. According to Uncle Eric, the _________ and _______ that led to World War I are highly important regarding the study of the First World War.

4. According to Uncle Eric, what is the cause of World War II?

5. According to Uncle Eric, what are the most important parts of World War II?

6. According to Uncle Eric, why are these the most important parts of World War II?

7. Uncle Eric tells the reader how far, chronologically, he plans to go in this set of letters about World War I. Chronologically, when will Uncle Eric begin his next set of letters on World War II?

8. According to Uncle Eric, what are the ten deadly ideas that lead to war?

9. How many wars have humans inflicted on themselves?

10. According to Uncle Eric, what caused "Old World" wars to become "World" Wars?

11. What is the economic lesson taught by Henry Hazlitt?

12. Applying Henry Hazlitt's economic lesson, what is the economic connection of the ten deadly ideas that lead to war?

Chapter 5: Whose Truth?

Define

1. Objective:

2. Subjective:

3. Federalist:

4. Anti-federalist:

Short Answer/Fill-In/True or False

5. What is the main point in the chapter titled, "Whose Truth"?

6. What question does Uncle Eric encourage Chris to always ask in the quest for truth?

7. According to the U.S. government, America's involvement in the World Wars was ____________.

For Research and Discussion

8. In a previous exercise you were asked to research World War I posters and World War II posters. Review those posters again. As you look at each poster, answer the following questions: What do you think the artist who created each poster is trying to make you think? In your opinion, how did the artist achieve his/her objectives through the art presented on the poster?

9. Is it customary for a writer to disclose his/her viewpoint? Make a list of the titles of some of your history books, both historical fiction and nonfiction titles. In another column list the viewpoint that the author discloses to the reader. If no viewpoint is disclosed, list "none." What conclusion/s can you draw from your findings?

Activity

10. According to Uncle Eric, Wilhelm Schurmann, a German professor of photography, points out that a photograph is never objective, but always subjective. An individual takes a photo and wants you to have some kind of reaction to it. A good example of this is the book MANZANAR by John Armor and Peter Wright, commentary by John Hersey, and photographs by Ansel Adams. It is published by Vintage Books, a division of Random House, New York. It is difficult to locate so check with your library or the internet and try to locate a copy. Adams was forbidden to photograph the guard towers, the guards, or the barbed wire, but Adams cleverly worked all three into his photographs. (Another source for Ansel Adams'

photographs of Japanese-American Internment at Manzanar can be found on the Internet: http://memory.loc.gov/ammem/aamhtml/)

If you have access to a camera, take a photograph in an effort to elicit a preconceived response/emotion from anyone who will view your photo. After the photograph is developed, ask several people to view your photo and let you know what they think/feel? Did they see and feel what you intended? If not, what might you do next time to more successfully achieve your goal?

(If you do not have access to a camera, alternate approaches for this activity might be to create a drawing, painting, or a collage.)

11. Draw, paint, or paste pictures to create a recruitment poster. After you complete the poster, write down what you want someone to feel when they view it. Ask members of your family, your friends, or neighbors to look at your poster and tell you what they feel. Based on their responses, did you achieve your goal? (If you do not wish to create a poster of your own, you can use World War I or World War II posters for this exercise and ask others what they feel and/or think when they view the posters.)

12. In the book, LOOK-ALIKES: DISCOVER A LAND WHERE THINGS ARE NOT AS THEY APPEAR... artist Joan Steiner uses everything from acorns to yardsticks to zippers, to create her three-dimensional world where everyday things look like what they're not. The harder you look, the more you'll find. Wonderful point of view book. When you've finished, make your own look-alike. (LOOK-ALIKES by Joan Steiner, published by Little, Brown & Co, Canada, 1998)

For Further Reading

13. Another excellent point of view book for young children is IT LOOKS LIKE THIS by Irma E. Webber. This book was originally written during World War II, which is why the text is black and white only; colored inks weren't available. The aim of the book is to show how someone can disagree with others about what he/she sees because each individual views something from his/her own unique point of view. It's a very good story. It has been out of print, but you may find it in the library or used on the Internet.

Chapter 6: Why We Fight

Define

1. Propaganda:

2. Foreign policy:

Short Answer/Fill-In/True or False

3. According to Uncle Eric, what is the message in the film WHY WE FIGHT? (Note: alternate films to view for this exercise might be:
VICTORY AT SEA (original to television)
ON THE FRONT LINES by Walt Disney Treasures, ISBN 0-7888-5070-9.)

To View

4. Watch several different war movies about World War I and World War II. Several are listed at the end of this study guide. For each movie:
   a. List the release date.
   b. Describe the emotions you feel as you listen to the music.
   c. Describe how the movie makes you feel about America and its soldiers.
   d. How does the movie make you feel about the enemy?
   e. List the causes for which the soldiers are fighting (both sides).

Chapter 7: Conquest Creates Weakness, Not Strength

Define

1. Occupy:

2. Division:

3. Kremlin:

Short Answer/Fill-In/True or False

4. True or False: Taking territory makes an army stronger.

Chapter 8: Typical Garden-Variety Wars

Define

1. Axis:

2. Allies:

3. Central Powers:

Short Answer/Fill-In/True or False

4. Do you agree or disagree with Uncle Eric that the best way to measure evil is by the number of innocent people murdered? Support your position.

Chapter 9. Deadly Ideas Lead to War

Short Answer/Fill-In/True or False

1. Before you read the chapter titled "Deadly Ideas Lead to War", comment on the following statement: Humans choose to go to war because of the ideas they hold. Explain your answer and include the ideas you think humans might hold that could lead them to choose to go to war. Retain this paper. Compare your ideas to the ideas that Uncle Eric will discuss as you proceed to read this chapter and the rest of this book.

2. Compare your list of deadly ideas to Uncle Eric's list.

Chapter 10: Pax Romana

Define

1. Pax Romana:

Short Answer/Fill-In/True or False

2. What is the Pax Romana myth?

3. How does the Pax Romana myth affect people today?

Chapter 11: Fascism

Define

1. Fascism:

Short Answer/Fill-In/True or False

2. Geographically, where was the Roman government strongest?

3. The Pax Romana myth became entrenched in __________ because the Roman government was strongest in __________.

4. For approximately nine centuries who were the two dominant powers in Europe?

5. What countries were the battlegrounds between these two large empires?

6. A ________ was the symbol of the ancient Roman political philosophy called fascism.

7. Describe what the symbol of fascism looked like and explain its symbolism.

8. True or False: The French and Austro-Hungarian use of fasces showed they wanted to unify the world under one government.

9. What is Uncle Eric's key point about fascism?

10. What happened in World War II to change people's opinions about fascism?

11. Explain the second deadly idea that leads to war as it pertains to fascism.

12. What is the truth about fascism in Europe?

13. Why were Hitler and Mussolini so popular?

Chapter 12: What Date Did the World Wars Begin?

Define

1. Neutrality:

Short Answer/Fill-In/True or False

2. According to Uncle Eric, when did the World Wars really begin and why?

3. What date do most historians identify as the start of the two World Wars?

4. Has peace been the exception or the rule in the Old World?

5. What advice did America's Founders give Americans regarding political connections with the Old World? What were their reasons?

6. Explain the difference, if any, between an isolationist and non-interventionist.

Chapter 13: Franco-Prussian War

Define

1. Alliances:

2. Reparations:

Short Answer/Fill-In/True or False

3. Uncle Eric says that the history of Europe's wars is a history of shifting alliances. Why is this information important?

4. On what date was the German Empire proclaimed?

Discussion/Essay/Assignment

5. Do you think the U.S. government is starting to emulate the behaviors of the Old World? Explain your answer.

Chapter 14: Ancient German Ambitions

Short Answer/Fill-In/True or False

1. In what year did Germany became a country?

2. Where and when did Prussia originate?

3. When did Prussia extend to the Rhine River?

4. Who first attempted to kill Adolph Hitler?

5. The ____________ and ______________________ were the source of most of the worst warfare since the Middle Ages.

6. Before reading the next chapter about the third deadly idea that leads to war, political power, answer the following three questions based on your current knowledge and/or opinions. Save your answers. After you have answered the questions, read Chapter 15 "Political Power."

    a. Define: Political power

    b. How do you know a government is a government?

    c. What makes government different from businesses, churches, charities, and other "private" organizations?

Chapter 15: Political Power

Short Answer/Fill-In/True or False

1. Political power is the __________ ______________ of using force on persons who have not harmed anyone.

2. What is Uncle Eric's definition of government?

3. According to Uncle Eric, what makes government different from other private institutions?

Discussion/Essay/Assignment

4. Uncle Eric asks, "Can you think of any situation in which government's decisions are not backed by force or threats of force?" Provide examples to support your answer.

5. Select one of the following quotes. Use it as the basis for a discussion or short essay in which you agree or disagree with the author of the quote. Explain your position.

    a. "Government is not reason; it is not eloquence; it is force. Like fire, it is a dangerous servant and a fearful master." —George Washington

    b. "Society in every state is a blessing, but government, even in its best state is but a necessary evil; in its worst state, an intolerable one. —Thomas Paine

    c. "I am more and more convinced that man is a dangerous creature; and that power, whether vested in many or a few, is ever grasping, and, like the grave, cries 'Give, give.'" —Abigail Adams

    d. "An honest man can feel no pleasure in the exercise of power over his fellow citizens." —Thomas Paine

6. Uncle Eric states, "the love of power is probably the main driving force behind wars." Do you agree or disagree and why?

7. Review your answers to question #6 from Chapter 14. After reading this chapter about political power, would you change any of your answers, and if so, why?

8. Before reading about global protection, which is the fourth deadly idea that leads to war, answer the following question: Under what circumstances, if any, do you think American military forces should be sent to rescue American citizens who get into trouble while traveling abroad? Save your answer. You will be asked to revisit it.

Chapter 16: Global Protection

Define

1. Global protection:

Short Answer/Fill-In/True or False

2. When did the idea of global protection for Americans begin?

For Discussion

^ 18 yrs

3. If you are approaching the age when you will be eligible for military service, can you answer Uncle Eric's question: What would you be willing to die for?

4. Review your answer to question #8 from Chapter 15. After reading this chapter about global protection would you change your answer, and if so, why?

Chapter 17: Interests

Define

1. Interests:

2. Gunboat diplomacy:

Short Answer/Fill-In/True or False

3. By the year ________ the idea that the U.S. armed forces were strictly for defense of our homeland was gone.

Discussion/Essay/Assignment

4. Write your representative or senator in the U.S. Congress and ask him/her to define for you what is meant by the term "interests." Use one of the examples quoted by Uncle Eric in this chapter about "interests" or listen for current examples in speeches or press conferences given by a current politician.

5. Do you believe that the armed forces should only be used for defense of the homeland? Under what circumstances, if any, should the armed forces be used as a global rescue service to protect American "interests" abroad? Would you be willing to take travel risks and do business in strange, far off lands if no government safety net were available?

Chapter 18: Cost Externalization

Define

1. Cost externalization:

Short Answer/Fill-In/True or False

2. Uncle Eric says, "For persons inside their homeland, the police and military forces are pledged to protect them to the fullest extent possible. History is replete with examples of troops and police giving their lives to protect the innocent." Provide examples from modern history in which military forces were used to protect your homeland.

3. What is the U.S. policy regarding U.S. citizens traveling in foreign countries?

4. Does the U.S. strictly practice this policy? Support your answer with examples.

5. In the Middle Ages, how did business people use economics to determine where they would or would not conduct business?

6. How is cost externalization a reason why America gets into wars?

For Research

7. Travel warnings are issued when the State Department recommends that Americans avoid a certain country. Visit the State Department web site at http://www.travel.state.gov/travel/cis_pa_tw/tw/tw_1764.html

   How many countries are listed? Select a couple of the countries and read the travel warning that is posted about that country.

Chapter 19: Manifest Destiny

Define

1. Mamelukes:

2. Manifest Destiny:

3. Imperialist:

Discussion/Essay/Assignment

4. In 1845, a New York editor, John L. O'Sullivan, had written that it was "the fulfillment of our manifest destiny to overspread the continent allotted by Providence for the free development of our yearly expanding millions." Do you agree or disagree with this statement? Give your reasons.

Chapter 20: The Splendid Little War

Discussion/Essay/Assignment

1. At the Treaty of Paris on December 10, 1898, neither the Cubans nor the Filipinos were allowed to take part in the negotiations about their futures. Their homelands were simply annexed by Washington as the first parts of the new U.S. Empire. If you were Cuban or Filipino, how do you think you might feel about the United States and Americans who won this "splendid little war?"

2. Select from either the Albright or Mencken statements that follow, and explain why you agree or disagree with the statement.

   a. Madeline Albright referred to America as "the indispensable nation." Under the doctrine of Indispensable Nation, the widely held belief in Washington is that Americans have the right and duty to intervene in other nations.

   b. H.L Mencken said, "The urge to save humanity is almost always a false-face for the urge to rule it."

Chapter 21: Guerrilla War

Define

1. Battalion:

Short Answer/Fill-In/True or False

2. True or False: Most wars today are guerrilla wars.

3. True or False: Uncle Eric says that the events that led to World War I are more important than events during the war.

4. What nation has the best track record for staying out of wars?

5. What is a regular troop?

6. What are militia?

7. What is a guerrilla?

8. What are the key points to the success of the guerrilla fighter?

9. Among military experts, what is the ratio of conventional troops to guerrilla fighters.

Discussion/Essay/Assignment

10. According to Uncle Eric, why is the Second Amendment in the Constitution? Do you agree or disagree with Uncle Eric, and why?

11. Can you remember ever studying or reading about a situation reported by an historian in which people found ways to stay out of wars? If so, give examples.

For Further Reading

12. Read more about revolutionary guerrilla Francis Marion, the Swamp Fox, through a biography, encyclopedia, or another source.

Chapter 22: Guerrilla War Examples

Short Answer/Fill-In/True or False

1. Who are militia-guerrillas trained to target? Why is this important?

2. Is a militia defensive or offensive?

3. What is the point to the William Tell story as told by the Swiss?

4. Are the American armed forces defensive or offensive?

Discussion/Essay/Assignment

5. What is your opinion of Uncle Eric's description of a militia: "A militia is a military version of the volunteer firefighters who are always trained and ready to turn out to fight fires."

6. U.S. history books praise the Minutemen (the militia from the American Revolutionary War). In Switzerland today, each member of the Swiss militia trains regularly, much like the National Guard in the U.S. He keeps his battle rifle and ammunition in his home ready for immediate use. Many people today do not believe ordinary citizens should own weapons. How do you feel about this issue? Write an essay supporting your position.

7. The purpose of the Supreme Court is to interpret the Constitution. If you were a Supreme Court judge, how would you interpret the following two amendments to the U.S. Constitution?

   The Second Amendment: "A well regulated militia, being necessary to the security of a free State, the right of the people to keep and bear arms, shall not be infringed."

   The Tenth Amendment: "The powers not delegated to the United States by the Constitution, nor prohibited by it to the states, are reserved to the states respectively, or the people."

8. After reading the chapters on guerrilla warfare, Switzerland, and snipers, would you vote for or against a law that said it would be okay for U.S. soldiers to assassinate foreign rulers? Explain your position.

For Further Reading

9. Read FEDERALIST PAPERS #20, #42 and #43. Check with a reference librarian or you can find them on the Internet at: http://www.yale.edu/lawweb/avalon/federal/fed.htm

Chapter 23: Never Surrender

Short Answer/Fill-In/True or False

1. List some of the characteristics of guerrillas.

2. Why is a central authority a convenience to the enemy?

Discussion/Essay/Assignment

3. In World War II, members of the Swiss militia took an oath never to surrender—no matter what their government might be forced to say or do. What are the similarities and differences between Swiss militia and the terrorists who attacked the World Trade Center on September 11, 2001?

Chapter 24: Killing Women

Short Answer/Fill-In/True or False

1. What is a consequence on the regular troops of fighting a guerrilla war?

2. What is the key to success for a guerrilla fighter?

3. The U.S. conquest of ____________________ was a crucial step toward the World Wars.

Chapter 25: Take No Prisoners

Define

1. Take No Prisoners:

Short Answer/Fill-In/True or False

2. According to Uncle Eric, what was the outcome of the war in the Philippines so far as U.S. government policy was concerned?

Chapter 26: The White Man's Burden and the Ugly American

Define

1. White Man's Burden:

2. Anglo-Saxonism:

3. Barbarian:

Short Answer/Fill-In/True or False

4. What is Washington's burden?

5. What did the United Nation's Human Rights Committee do to the U.S. government in 2001 and why?

For Further Reading

6. Read Rudyard Kipling's poem, "The White Man's Burden." What was Kipling's message? The poem can be found on the Internet at: http://www.fordham.edu/halsall/mod/Kipling.html

To View or For Further Reading

7. Watch the movie "The Ugly American" (or read the book by the same title). What does the "Ugly American" refer to?

Chapter 27: The Great White Fleet

Short Answer/Fill-In/True or False

1. Why did Theodore Roosevelt send his Great White Fleet of 16 new battleships around the world in 1907?
2. Who was the undisputed industrial leader of the world by the 1890s?
3. From the time of the Great White Fleet on, what was clear to every other government in the world?
4. Why does Uncle Eric believe that the Spanish-American War and conquest of the Philippines are the most important conflicts the U.S. has ever fought?

Discussion/Essay/Assignment

5. Uncle Eric asks, "Consider the difference between the Great White Fleet and the Swiss militiaman. Which type of military power do you think is more ethical?"

Chapter 28: Up Close and Personal

Define

1. Area bombing:
2. Delayed stress syndrome:
3. Fragging:

Short Answer/Fill-In/True or False

4. Uncle Eric makes the point that the more geographically distanced a soldier is from the enemy, the more detached he/she becomes from the psychological toll of killing people. What effect, if any, do you think long-range missiles that can travel hundreds of miles will have on soldiers?

Chapter 29: The First Casualty of War

Define

1. War fever:

Discussion/Essay/Assignment

2. Explain why you agree or disagree with the following statement made by Senator Hiram Johnson in 1917: "The first casualty when war comes is truth."

3. Make a list of past and current news stories that were reported as fact but later were announced as incorrect. For example, one media error was the announcement that the state of Florida had gone to Al Gore early on election night in the November 2000 presidential election.

4. What might you do to guard against war fever?

Chapter 30: Stealing Panama

Short Answer/Fill-In/True or False

1. After the Spanish-American War and conquest of the Philippines, what practice regarding American military personnel was solidly entrenched?

2. What was the next noteworthy military incident after the Spanish-American war?

Chapter 31: Helping Crooks and Tyrants

Define

1. Fungible:

Short Answer/Fill-In/True or False

2. What is Uncle Eric's point regarding the protections of the Constitution and Bill of Rights?

Discussion/Essay/Assignment

3. Uncle Eric says, "During the 20th century, every president sent American troops to far corners of the globe, usually not to defend liberty but to train, equip, or provide other kinds of help to the armed forces of crooks and tyrants. These crooks and tyrants have included, but are not limited to: President Diem of Vietnam, the Shah of Iran, Marcos in the Philippines, Manuel Noriega in Panama, Saddam Hussein in Iraq, Mobutu in the Congo, Chiang Kai-shek in Taiwan, General Park in Korea, and Suharto and Habibie in Indonesia." Research the biographies of these crooks and tyrants, Chris, and remember, they all received help from Washington." Read/research about one of these persons.

4. Uncle Eric further states that the military assistance received is usually used to suppress a tyrant's own people. The Shah of Iran and his secret police, for instance, terrorized Iranians for 25 years with the backing of the U.S. government. Do you think the peoples of these lands like or dislike America? To what extent?

5. What is the danger of helping other tyrannical governments nonmilitarily?

6. Uncle Eric says, "There are about 220 countries in the world. As I write this, the USG has 280,000 troops stationed in 138 of them, from Antigua to Zimbabwe, about two-thirds of all countries. All these American troops are providing some kind of help to the governments of these countries. All these governments have enemies, so now their enemies are our enemies." Read the excerpt from George Washington's Farewell Address from page two of WORLD WAR I. What does Washington say about getting involved in the affairs of Europe? What conclusion does Uncle Eric draw for the September 11, 2001 attack against the United States?

For Research

7. Uncle Eric says, "A good research project is to look up the assistance, especially military aid, provided to other governments, then look up the amount of freedom these governments allow. You might start with the STATISTICAL ABSTRACT OF THE UNITED STATES, and for the amount of freedom, check the Freedom Scale on the Freedom House web site, and the Index of Economic Freedom on the Heritage Foundation web site."
For the aid: Amnesty International web site:
www.amnestyusa.org/arms_trade/controlarms_summary.html

   State Department:
   www.state.gov/g/drl/rls/hrrpt/2001

   Freedom House web site: www.freedomhouse.org

   Index of Economic Freedom: www.heritage.org/research/features/index

   Several countries are listed in Richard Maybury's book WHATEVER HAPPENED TO PENNY CANDY, 4th and 5th editions, which includes the country's index of freedom and its legal system. (WHATEVER HAPPENED TO PENNY CANDY is published by Bluestocking Press, www.BluestockingPress.com.)

For Further Reading

8. Read Dr. Seuss' anti-fascist story YERTLE THE TURTLE, published by Random House. As you read it, ponder this question: What is the point of having political power if you cannot use it on someone?

Chapter 32: The Usual Suspects

Short Answer/Fill-In/True or False

1. Make a list of the Usual Suspects that are generally involved when a war breaks out.

2. What criteria does Uncle Eric use to place a government on the list of Usual Suspects?

For Research

3. Think of the major wars throughout history. Imagine yourself as a law enforcement officer and ask: Which of the Usual Suspects was behind each of the wars you are researching? Check the history of the people who are fighting.

Chapter 33: Boxer Rebellion and Russo-Japanese War

Define

1. Yihequan:

Short Answer/Fill-In/True or False

2. Where did the name Boxer come from?

3. What is significant about the Russo-Japanese war?

For Research

4. Uncle Eric suggests you always ask, "Who is on whose territory" when a war is being fought? As you continue to study history, keep a list of who is on whose territory.

Chapter 34: Choosing Up Sides

Short Answer/Fill-In/True or False

1. Who said, "A generation that has taken a beating is always followed by a generation that deals one"?

2. What alliance became the cornerstone of what would eventually become the Central Powers in World War I?

3. What three countries formed the so-called Triple Alliance in World War I?

4. What three countries formed the core of the Central Powers in World War I?

5. What three countries formed the core of the Axis in World War II?

6. What country switched sides in both World Wars?

7. What three countries formed the core of the Allies in World War I?

8. What three countries formed the core of the Allies in World War II?

For Research

9. On the internet, Worldpress.org (www.worldpress.org) reports that as of September 2003, "at least 35 countries were in some stage of major armed conflict, from tenuous cease-fire to all-out war." Select one country that is involved in armed conflict. Determine if the current generation that is taking the beating is being dealt that beating by its enemies from the previous generation. If the data is available, are you able to determine how many generations are involved in the war you are researching? Report your findings.

To View

10. THE ADVENTURES OF YOUNG INDIANA JONES: DEMONS OF DECEPTION. Film looks at the horrors of war and the callousness of politicians. Does an excellent job of explaining the alliances and the reasons that led to World War I.

Chapter 35: The Morocco Crisis

Short Answer/Fill-In/True or False

1. Identify the two deadly ideas that led to the Morocco crisis.

2. How did the Germans acquire land in Black equatorial Africa?

3. Were the Africans in Black equatorial Africa asked if they wanted to be ruled by Germany? What might be the result of this type of land exchange?

Chapter 36: Alliances

Short Answer/Fill-In/True or False

1. What is the lesson to be learned from World War I about alliances as taught by Uncle Eric?

2. What small war became World War I because of alliances?

3. Which country had avoided military alliances for nearly two centuries?

4. According to Uncle Eric, what led to the September 11, 2001 attacks and the war that followed?

Chapter 37: The Glory of War

Define

1. Trench sweeper:

2. The Great War:

Short Answer/Fill-In/True or False

3. What weapon changed the face of war and helped create conditions that led to the Treaty of Versailles, which led to World War II?

Discussion/Essay/Assignment

4. Do you agree or disagree with Uncle Eric's statement, "Weapons are just tools, and like a hammer, knife, or chain saw, they can be used for good or evil." Explain.

For Research

5. Using a dictionary and/or encyclopedia, make a list of the types of diseases that resulted from trench warfare. An Internet site for trench warfare is: http://www.spartacus.schoolnet.co.uk/FWWtrench.htm

6. Research the types of weaponry that were introduced in World War I.

Chapter 38: America's Entry Into World War I

Short Answer/Fill-In/True or False

1. In 1914 Germany was __________ years old.
2. When was the German Empire proclaimed?
3. According to Uncle Eric, how did Germany build its new empire?
4. What nations regarded Germany as an aggressor?
5. How did smaller countries become involved in wars?
6. How far did the battle line between France and Germany move during the course of World War I?
7. True or False: When World War I erupted, President Wilson had declared that the U.S. would remain neutral.
8. What deadly idea that leads to war was exemplified by the sinking of the *Lusitania*?
9. According to Uncle Eric, on April 6, 1917, who saved the war and how?
10. What caused World War I to become a global war?

Discussion/Essay/Assignment

11. Discuss how far removed or how closely tied America is today to the original founding American principles: liberty, free markets, and international neutrality. Support your position.

For Research

12. Uncle Eric asks Chris to check encyclopedias or a library database under the search words British Empire, Russian Empire and French Empire. Then look for German Empire. Compare the amount of information available for each.

Chapter 39: The Third Choice Ignored

Short Answer/Fill-In/True or False

1. When did Germany surrender?

Discussion/Essay/Assignment

2. Write an essay on the differences or similarities among the following terms: isolationism, noninterventionism, interventionism, neutrality. Which position best represents your own personal philosophy? Explain.

3. What responsibility does the media have to accurately report news? In your opinion, does the media today report the news or create the news? Or, both? Explain your answer.

4. Try to secure a copy of DR. SEUSS GOES TO WAR: THE WORLD WAR II EDITORIAL CARTOONS OF THEODOR SEUSS GEISEL, text and compilation by Richard H. Minear, published by The New Press, NY, copyright 1999.
   An Internet site for Geisel's editorial cartoons is: http://orpheus.ucsd.edu/speccoll/dspolitic/
   Geisel was against isolationism and many of his editorial cartoons reflect his bias. What effect might this type of editorializing have on his readers?

5. In this chapter Uncle Eric talks about the propaganda posters.
   On the Internet visit: www.WorldPress.org
   Click on the link to "World in Cartoons" for contemporary international political cartoons. You will very likely see some that are not favorable to U.S. foreign policy. Discuss some of these cartoons with your teacher. How does it make you feel to see the perspective from foreign presses on the U.S. government?

6. Reporters are embedded with soldiers who are fighting the War on Terror. What responsibility should embedded reporters have in reporting their stories? What are the pros and cons of using embedded soldiers? If still posted on the Internet, visit:
   http://www.worldpress.org/eduView.cfm/hurl/id=37
   Read the information provided to help you with your essay. If it is no longer posted, do an Internet search to learn more about the topic of embedded reporters.

For Further Reading

7. To learn about crowd mentality, read EXTRAORDINARY POPULAR DELUSIONS AND THE MADNESS OF CROWDS by Charles Mackay, published by Crown Publishers, New York.

Chapter 40: They Will Fight Over Anything

Short Answer/Fill-In/True or False

1. According to Uncle Eric, what caused the wars of Europe and Asia to become World Wars?

Chapter 41: The Treaty of Versailles

Define

1. *Lebensraum*:

Short Answer/Fill-In/True or False

2. Uncle Eric says the U.S. government and Hollywood tend to see things in terms of good guys versus bad guys. Who were the good guys in World War I?
3. True or False: The Allied rulers blamed the First World War on the German government as well as the German people.
4. Why did economist John Maynard Keynes quit the conference at which the Treaty of Versailles was being drafted?
5. When did Hitler invade Poland?
6. What are the essential chain of events in World War I that led to World War II?

Discussion/Essay/Assignment

7. As you listen to news reports and political speeches and watch Hollywood films or television shows that address the topic of the War on Terror, determine if the U.S. government and Hollywood still tend to see things in terms of good guys versus bad guys as Uncle Eric says was done in the World Wars of the 20th century.

Chapter 42: The Sound of Reloading

Short Answer/Fill-In/True or False

1. What marked the end of World War I and the beginning of World War II?
2. What caused the Germans to begin rearming?

Chapter 43: Hitler's Rise

Define

1. League of Nations:
2. Nationalism:
3. Aryan race:

Short Answer/Fill-In/True or False

4. When did Adolph Hitler get his start?
5. How did the German government find the money to pay its penalties?
6. Who did the German people believe was responsible for their deprivation?
7. When did Adolph Hitler become leader of the Nazi Party?
8. Nazism was a form of what "ism?"
9. In what year did the Nazi Party try to take over the government of the German state of Bavaria? What happened to Hitler as a result?
10. What famous book did Hitler write while in prison?
11. What is Hitler's famous book about?
12. How did the U.S. government try to help the German government pay its reparations?
13. Where else did the U.S. expanded money supply go and what was the result?
14. What caused the beginning of the 1929 Great Depression?
15. Was the depression restricted to the U.S.?
16. What major nation was hit hardest by the depression?

For Further Reading

17. To learn more about "isms" read the chapter titled "Capitalism and Other Isms" in Karl Hess' book CAPITALISM FOR KIDS published by Bluestocking Press, web site: www.BluestockingPress.com, phone: 800-959-8586. Be sure to note the differences between communism and totalitarianism.

Chapter 44: U.S. Invades Russia

Define

1. Cossacks:

Short Answer/Fill-In/True or False

2. The U.S. invaded Russia in ____________.

3. Under what deadly idea did the U.S. invade Russia?

4. When did the Cold War begin?

5. Why did the Russians not trust the U.S.?

Discussion/Essay/Assignment

6. Uncle Eric suggests that you ask people the following question: "Has the U.S. ever invaded Russia." If they answer "yes," ask for details. For example, does the person know when the U.S. invaded Russia and why?

For Research

7. Uncle Eric says that several governments did not want the Bolsheviks in power. However, they also did not know who they did want in power. In 2001 as the Taliban government began to fall in Afghanistan, a similar problem faced the U.S. and its Allies. Who is currently the recognized government of Afghanistan? Who is the recognized government of Iraq?

To View

8. DOCTOR ZHIVAGO starring Omar Sharif and Julie Christie. Spans several decades including WWI and the Bolshevik Revolution.

Chapter 45: Desperation and the Neutrality Act

Define

1. Conscription:

Short Answer/Fill-In/True or False

2. Why did Hitler become popular in Germany?
3. In what month and year did the Nazi Party take control of the German government?
4. When was the first concentration camp erected and where?
5. When did Hitler proclaim himself Fuhrer?
6. Hitler set up a command economy. What is a command economy and what was the result?
7. What were the German businesses and workers producing?
8. When did Hitler introduce conscription?
9. Explain the Neutrality Act passed by the U.S. Congress in March 1935.
10. What does Uncle Eric consider the greatest mistake in morals and judgment and a violation of America's founding principles?

For Further Reading

11. To learn more about the economics behind the German runaway inflation, read the chapter titled "Wallpaper, Wheelbarrows and Recessions" from the book WHATEVER HAPPENED TO PENNY CANDY? by Richard J. Maybury, published by Bluestocking Press, web site: BluestockingPress.com, phone: 800-959-8586.

Chapter 46: Summary

Short Answer/Fill-In/True or False

1. True or False: A fundamental belief of America's Founders was that political power corrupts the morals and the judgment.

2. True or False: According to America's Founders, the U.S. government should be able to grow as large as it possibly can so it can better exert its power.

3. True or False: In foreign affairs, George Washington believed that the U.S. government must be isolationist.

4. It was the ____________ government's participation in the garden-variety European and Asian wars that turned them into World Wars.

5. List the ten deadly ideas that lead to war.

6. The Second Amendment to the U.S. Constitution provides for a ____________________.

Discussion/Essay/Assignment

7. In this chapter, Uncle Eric recaps the ten deadly ideas that lead to war. Select one of the deadly ideas and write an essay in which you argue for or against the idea you select.

8. Uncle Eric says, "Whenever you see a film, listen to a political speech, or read an article or book, including this one, ask yourself, 'What is the writer's agenda? What does he want me to think?'" For the next four weeks, make a list of the films you view, the news articles you read, the books you read, and the speeches you hear. Next to the name/title of each, list the bias/philosophical slant of the author/commentator and/or what you think he/she is trying to get you to believe.

Thought Exercises Revisited

Before you began to read WORLD WAR I you were asked to provide answers to the following:

1. Write an essay on what patriotism means to you. Provide three examples from history in which individuals demonstrated through their actions your definition of patriotism.

2. Based on your current knowledge and opinions, write an essay detailing what caused World War I and World War II, what countries were on what side, who won, what were the results of the wars, etc.

3. What is the difference, if any, between international "neutrality" and "isolationism"?

Now that you have finished reading Richard J. Maybury's book WORLD WAR I, review your answers to the Thought Exercises. Would you make any changes to your answers? Explain what changes you would make and why. If you would make no changes, explain why you are satisfied with your answers as previously written. If you did not originally provide an answer for lack of knowledge, answer the exercises now.

Application Exercise

Complete and turn in your "Country in Armed Conflict" portfolio to your instructor at this time.

Final Exam

1. Define: Patriotism
2. Name the two laws that make civilization possible.
3. What did America's Founders believe about political power?
4. The ______________ government switched sides in World War I, starting the war on the side of the Central Powers and ending on the side of the Allies.
5. According to Uncle Eric, what is the cause of World War II?
6. Define: Propaganda
7. Define: Foreign policy
8. True or False: Taking territory makes an army stronger. Explain your answer.
9. Define: Axis
10. Define: Allies
11. Define: Central Powers
12. Define: Fascism
13. For approximately nine centuries who were the two dominant powers in Europe?
14. True or False: According to Uncle Eric, fascism was regarded as a respectable philosophy until World War II.
15. Define: Neutrality
16. Most historians say that the World Wars began in the year _______ with the ______________ War.
17. Explain the difference, if any, between an isolationist and non-interventionist.
18. Define: Alliances
19. Define: Reparations

20. The ______________ Empire was proclaimed on January 18, 1871, following the Franco-Prussian war.

21. The ____________ and ____________________ were the source of most of the worst warfare since the Middle Ages.

22. Define: Political power

23. Define: Global protection

24. The idea of global protection for Americans began during the __________________ Wars.

25. By the year ________ the idea that the U.S. armed forces were strictly for defense of our homeland was gone.

26. Define: Cost externalization

27. True or False: Most wars today are guerrilla wars.

28. ____________________ is the nation that has the best track record for staying out of wars.

29. What are three key points to the success of the guerrilla fighter?

30. Who are militia-guerrillas trained to target? Why is this important?

31. Is a militia defensive or offensive?

32. Are the American armed forces defensive or offensive?

33. Why is a central authority a convenience to the enemy?

34. Who was the undisputed industrial leader of the world by the 1890s?

35. After the Spanish-American War and conquest of the Philippines, what practice regarding American military personnel was solidly entrenched?

36. Name the Usual Suspects that are generally involved when a war breaks out.

37. What is significant about the Russo-Japanese war?

38. The ______________ and the _____________ formed an alliance that became the cornerstone of what would eventually become the Central Powers in World War I.

39. One of the most important lessons to learn from World War I is that __________________ turn small wars into big ones.

40. What weapon changed the face of war and helped create conditions that led to the Treaty of Versailles, which led to World War II?

41. How far did the battle line between France and Germany move during the course of World War I?

42. True or False: When World War I erupted, President Wilson had declared that the U.S. would remain neutral.

43. What caused World War I to become a global war?

44. When did Germany surrender?

45. True or False: The Allied rulers blamed the First World War on the German government as well as the German people.

46. According to Uncle Eric, what are the four essential chain of events in World War I that led to World War II?

47. What marked the end of World War I and the beginning of World War II?

48. What caused the Germans to begin rearming?

49. In what month and year did the Nazi Party take control of the German government?

50. List the ten deadly ideas that lead to war.

Essay: Several comments/quotes about World War I are listed in the Appendix of Richard J. Maybury's book WORLD WAR I. These also appear in this study guide beginning on page 90. Richard Maybury said, *"Each of these comments makes a point that can be used for discussion or research. Is the point true, what do you think?"* For this essay, select one of the comments/quotes from the list provided. Do you agree or disagree with the perspective provided? If possible, support your position with points or examples provided by Uncle Eric in Richard J. Maybury's book WORLD WAR I.

Essay: Listed on pages 94 and 95 of this study guide are three quotes, one from George Washington and two from Thomas Jefferson. Select one of these quotes. Explain why you agree or disagree with the author of the quote you selected. Provide support for your position.

Answers

Uncle Eric's Model of How the World Works

Short Answer/Fill-in/True or False

1. Uncle Eric says that models are how we think. They are how we understand how the world works.

2. According to Uncle Eric, models are important because we constantly refer to our models to help us determine what incoming data is important and what data is not.

3. It is important to sort incoming data because we need to decide what incoming data we need to remember or file for future reference, and what data we can discard, based on its importance to us, or its usefulness. We need a tool for making this determination. That tool is also called our "model."

4. This answer requires the student to draw his/her own conclusion based on the information provided in the explanation of "Uncle Eric's Model of How the World Works." Possible answer: We should always be willing to test our models against incoming data, and if our models don't stand up to the incoming data, then it becomes necessary to question and perhaps rethink our model, as well as question the reliability of the incoming data.

5. Free market economics and Higher Law are the two models Uncle Eric thinks are most reliable, as well as crucially important for everyone to learn. Free market economics and Higher Law are important models because they show how human civilization works, especially the world of money.

6. **Fascism** is the political philosophy that is no philosophy at all. It embraces the concept that those in power can do whatever appears necessary to achieve their goals.

Discussion/Essay/Assignment

7. Examples of models will vary and might include scientific models, religious models, economic models, political models, etc.

8. The book WORLD WAR I explains how the U.S. government's involvement in the wars of Europe and Asia turned them into World Wars. By examining the wars through the eyes of Uncle Eric, readers have an opportunity to test the model they have previously used for studying the World Wars to see if their model stands up to the economic, legal, and historical data presented through Uncle Eric's letters.

9. Answers will vary.

10. Look at the front matter of your dictionary. There should be an explanation of the "Order of Definitions." For example, the order of definitions can be historical order: the earliest meaning is placed first and later meanings are arranged by semantic development.

11. The reader must understand what the author means by the words the author uses so the reader can understand the progression of the author's ideas that build on the definition of the terms used. This does not require that a reader agree with the author's definition of a word, only that the reader understand what the author means when the author uses the word. Then the reader is in a better position to critically examine the author's ideas based on a common understanding of the author's meaning.

12. Answers will vary, but might include some of the following explanations: Definitions provide clear understanding and communication between the parties involved. For example, suppose you eat a piece of fruit. This fruit happens to be a banana. Someone comes along who has never before seen or tasted a banana. With the banana in your presence, you can each begin to discuss its merits, and you will each know exactly what you're talking about. As in the Richard Feynman example, you are understanding the characteristics of the banana that go into making up what that "thing" is. To be able to give the "thing" a name, banana, that both parties can use in future communication will help promote speedier and clearer communication. This is the purpose of always making sure that you understand the definition of a term used in a discussion (whether in conversation or in books). You don't have to agree with the person's definition, but if you understand what the person means by it, you can have a clearer and more meaningful discussion instead of getting bogged down in misunderstandings regarding fuzzy language.

Author's Disclosure

Short Answer/Fill-in/True or False

1. Juris Naturalism is the belief in a Natural Law that is higher than any government's law.

Discussion/Essay/Assignment

2. Answers will vary, but students should note that the bias or philosophical slant of an author, news commentator, or reporter can influence the selection of facts included in a book or report, thereby slanting the history, or other subject areas.

3. Answers will vary.
4. Answers will vary.
5. Answers will vary.
6. Answers will vary.

Thought Exercises

Save the responses to all Thought Exercises. Students will be asked to revisit these questions and their answers.

1-3. Answers will vary, but should show thought and logic.

Dedication

1. Answers will vary.

Cast of Characters

1. Essays will vary.

2. During WWI few women were in positions of power.

3. *Allies —World War I*
(enemies of the Central Powers)
Belgium
Great Britain
U.S.
Russia
Greece
France
Japan
Italy
China
Brazil
Montenegro
Portugal
Romania

Allies—World War II
(enemies of the Axis)
Great Britain
U.S.
Russia

Central Powers – World War I
(enemies of the Allies)
Germany
Austria-Hungary
Turkey
Bulgaria

Axis—World War II
(enemies of the Allies)
Germany
Italy
Japan
Bulgaria
Finland
Hungary
Romania

Chapter 1: The 58-Year Persecution

Define

1. Patriotism. Dedication to the principles on which the country was founded, and a willingness to stand firm and fight for these principles regardless of what the government says or does.

2. Economics. The study of the production and distribution of goods and services.

Short Answer/Fill-In/True or False

3. Uncle Eric begins with events leading not to World War II, but to World War I, because his research and study has caused him to view World War II as chapter two of World War I.

4. According to Uncle Eric, the greatest weakness in education today is that connections, as well as political and economic history, are seldom taught in schools. Subjects are compartmentalized. Educators tend to teach as they were taught and most of them were taught the same compartmentalized approach to history. The lack of connections and the lack of political and economic history reinforce a student's tendency to see only one side of the story about the World Wars as well as all of America's wars.

   Answers as to whether the student agrees or disagrees as well as support for the student's position will vary.

5. The two laws that make civilization possible are: 1) Do all you have agreed to do, and 2) do not encroach on other persons or their property.

6. "Do all you have agreed to do" is the basis of contract law.

7. "Do not encroach on other persons or their property" is the basis of tort law and some criminal law.

8. Uncle Eric's approach to writing about the World Wars is to provide Chris with an explanation of the wars, not a description.

9. Uncle Eric's purpose in writing this series of letters about the World Wars is that he wants Chris to understand the wars so that Chris will not make uninformed decisions in his own life.

10. Uncle Eric's conclusions and observations are based on the principles taught by America's Founders. These principles taught by America's Founders are: liberty, free markets, international neutrality, and limited government.

11. America's Founders believed that political power corrupts the morals and the judgment and that no one can be trusted with it, so government must be kept very limited.

12. Uncle Eric says he will delve deeply into economics, which is rarely touched upon in other history books.

13. Answers will vary.

14. According to Uncle Eric, most of us have been taught that World War II military officers, not politicians, were at fault. We have generally been taught that if the military had done their job, the Japanese might have been beaten at Pearl Harbor.

15. Patriotism was prominently talked about and sung about following the September 11, 2001 attacks on the World Trade Center and Pentagon.

For Research and Discussion

16. Examples from U.S. or world history in which individuals or a group of individuals demonstrated through their actions that they chose country over their country's institutions or its officeholders include, but are not limited to: The U.S. Civil War (the South's reasons for secession). Individuals who transported slaves along the Underground Railroad. Individuals who hid Jews from the Nazis during World War II. The assassination attempt on Adolph Hitler by some of his own generals.

17. Examples of governments violating the two laws may include:

    Do not encroach on other people or their property.

    Japanese Internment during WWII
    confiscation of Native American lands
    confiscation of personal property through eminent domain
    confiscation of property owned by Jewish people by the Nazis
    genocide in various countries

    Do all you have agreed to do.

    Treaty violations

18. Examples from world and U.S. history in which governments have acted in unethical ways can include but are not limited to: mistreatment of prisoners of war, segregation because of race in the military, segregation of blacks in the South, confiscation of private lands to build dams, enslaving peoples who were captured during war.

19. Students should research other history textbooks at varying grade levels, as well as encyclopedias, and other reference sources.

20. Answers will vary.

Chapter 2: The Grim Statistics

Short Answer/Fill-In/True or False

1. The **Italian** government switched sides in World War I, starting the war on the side of the Central Powers and ending on the side of the Allies.

Assignment

2. Students should complete the exercise given: Per the suggestion in this chapter, locate each country on a globe or world map. Use the same colored marker to identify the nations that comprised the Allied Powers and a different colored marker to identify the nations that comprised the Central Powers.

Chapter 3: Is Now the Time to Learn About War?

Define

1. Statist. One who believes in a large, powerful central government and who believes that there is no law higher than the government's law.

2. Nonstatist. One who believes there is a higher law than any human law, and the government should be subject to this law and kept very limited.

For Research and Discussion

3. Answers will vary.

4. Answers will vary. Examples of slogans are:
   Be All That You Can Be...in the Army
   Join the Navy...See the World

Chapter 4: First Ideas, Then Battles

Define

1. Diplomacy. Communication and negotiations between governments.

2. Geopolitical. World political events, as opposed to national political events.

Short Answer/Fill-In/True or False

3. According to Uncle Eric, the **ideas** and **events** that led to World War I are highly important regarding the study of the First World War.

4. According to Uncle Eric, the cause of World War II is World War I.

5. According to Uncle Eric, the most important parts of World War II are the way the U.S. got into it: Pearl Harbor; and the way the war was conducted.

6. According to Uncle Eric, these are the most important parts of World War II because they set the stage for the world we live in today.

7. The set of letters on World War II will begin in the 1930s.

8. The ten deadly ideas that lead to war are: the Pax Romana, fascism, love of political power, global protection, interests, cost externalization, Manifest Destiny, alliances, the glory of war, and the White Man's Burden.

9. Humans have inflicted more than 14,000 wars on themselves.

10. The U.S. government's involvement in the wars of the Old World turned them into "World" Wars.

11. The economic lesson taught by Henry Hazlitt is: "The art of economics consists in looking not merely at the immediate but at the longer effects of any act or policy; it consists in tracing the consequences of that policy not merely for one group but for all groups."

12. The economic connection of the ten deadly ideas that lead to war is that each deadly idea has a consequence, not merely for one group, but for all groups.

Chapter 5: Whose Truth?

Define

1. Objective. Opposite of subjective. Having to do with a real object rather than an opinion. Being independent of the mind; real, actual, existing.

2. Subjective. Opposite of objective. Having to do with opinion rather than actual fact. Affected by the feelings or beliefs of the observer.

3. Federalist. One who advocated a strong central government for the U.S. An example was Alexander Hamilton.

4. Anti-federalist. One who opposed creation of the federal government. An example was Patrick Henry.

Short Answer/Fill-In/True or False

5. The main point in the chapter "Whose Truth" is: Books, movies, photos, and other mediums of communication are always produced by humans who use some viewpoint to select what they will present and what they will omit.

6. Uncle Eric encourages Chris to always ask, "What is this person trying to make me think?"

7. According to the U.S. government, America's involvement in the World Wars was **necessary.**

For Research and Discussion

8. Answers will vary based on the posters' subject matter.

9. Students' history book titles will vary but most should arrive at the same conclusion: It is not customary for an author to disclose his or her viewpoint.

Activity

10. Photos will vary, but students should be able to determine if they were successful in this project if those who viewed their photos elicited the response the student wanted.

11. Posters used will vary, but students should be able to determine if they were successful in this project if those who viewed their posters elicited the response the student wanted.

12. Student-created look-a-likes will vary.

For Further Reading

13. Optional exercise due to the limited availability of the title.

Chapter 6: Why We Fight

Define

1. Propaganda. Strongly biased information designed to persuade, usually relating to political or economic matters. The bias is often subtle and usually hidden and may make use of lies and half-truths.

2. Foreign policy. The government's behavior toward other governments and toward persons in other lands.

Short Answer/Fill-In/True or False

3. According to Uncle Eric, the message in the film WHY WE FIGHT is that America is good and because America is good it has the duty to send its young men and women to risk their lives fighting evil anywhere in the world.

To View

4. Answers will vary because file selections will vary.

Chapter 7: Conquest Creates Weakness, Not Strength

Define

1. Occupy. To station troops in a country to watch the conquered people and force them to obey the laws of the conqueror.

2. Division. Generally, six brigades. An infantry division is about 10,000 troops. An armored division, about 600 tanks. Typically, but not always, there are nine troops in a squad, three squads to a platoon, four platoons to a company, six companies to a battalion, two battalions to a brigade, and six brigades to a division.

3. Kremlin. A medieval fortified area in Moscow used as the center of the Russian government. The word is commonly used to mean the Russian government.

Short Answer/Fill-In/True or False

4. False. The correct answer is: Taking territory makes an army weaker because as an army advances it must leave troops behind to occupy the conquered areas. This reduces the number of troops that are left to fight at the front lines. If this continually happens, the army continues to weaken at the front lines, and it will start losing.

Chapter 8: Typical Garden-Variety Wars

Define

1. Axis. In World War II, the alliance led by Berlin, Rome, and Tokyo. Enemies of the Allies.

2. Allies. In World War I, the alliance led by London, Moscow, and Washington. Enemies of the Central Powers. In World War II, the same group; enemies of the Axis.

3. Central Powers. In World War I, the group led by Germany and Austria-Hungary. Consisted of Germany, the Austro-Hungarian Empire, Turkey, and Bulgaria. Enemies of the Allies.

Short Answer/Fill-In/True or False

4. Answers will vary.

Chapter 9: Deadly Ideas Lead to War

Short Answer/Fill-In/True or False

1. Papers will vary.

2. Student's list of ideas will vary.

    Uncle Eric's list
    1. Pax Romana
    2. Fascism
    3. Love of political power
    4. Global protection
    5. Interests
    6. Cost externalization
    7. Manifest Destiny
    8. Alliances
    9. The glory of war
    10. The White Man's Burden

Chapter 10: Pax Romana

Define

1. Pax Romana. The two centuries starting in 31 B.C., usually assumed to be a period of peace in the Roman Empire.

Short Answer/Fill-In/True or False

2. The Pax Romana myth says that for two centuries, beginning in 31 BC, the Roman Empire was peaceful and prosperous due to a huge, powerful central government that kept everyone in line.

3. The Pax Romana myth causes people to believe that a strong central government is necessary for peaceful times.

Chapter 11: Fascism

Define

1. Fascism. The political philosophy that is no philosophy at all. Do whatever appears necessary. It is derived from the law of the Roman Empire.

Short Answer/Fill-In/True or False

2. The Roman government was strongest in Europe.

3. The Pax Romana myth became entrenched in **Europe** because the Roman government was strongest in **Europe**.

4. For about nine centuries, the two dominant powers in Europe were the French Empire and the Austro-Hungarian Empire. The Austro-Hungarian Empire included the Holy Roman Empire and the Habsburg Empire.

5. Denmark, Germany, Switzerland, and Italy were the battlegrounds between these two large empires.

6. A **fasces** was the symbol of the ancient Roman political philosophy called fascism.

7. A fasces is a bundle of rods bound with an ax or spear. The bound rods symbolize all the people of all the provinces "unified" under a single government. The ax or spear symbolizes what would happen to anyone who did not obey this government.

8. True. The French and Austro-Hungarian use of fasces showed they wanted to unify the world under one government.

9. Uncle Eric's key point is that fascism was regarded as a respectable philosophy until World War II.

10. In the Second World War, dictators Hitler (Germany) and Mussolini (Italy) showed where fascism leads.

11. We are led to believe that fascism popped up suddenly in the 20th century, and World War II was a necessary sacrifice to stop fascism. This is the second deadly idea.

12. The truth about fascism in Europe is that fascism was quite popular among Europeans for some two thousand years and they practiced it widely against each other for many centuries as a way of creating a new Pax Romana.

13. Millions all over Europe already believed in fascism and Hitler and Mussolini were just trying to be more effective at it.

Chapter 12: What Date Did the World Wars Begin?

Define

1. Neutrality. Not aligned with, supporting, or favoring any side in a war or dispute.

Short Answer/Fill-In/True or False

2. According to Uncle Eric, the only logical place for the World Wars to begin was two thousand years ago in Ancient Rome because the two World Wars of the twentieth century were simply a continuation of European behavior—two more chapters in the ancient attempt to forcibly recreate the Pax Romana.

3. Most historians say that the World Wars began in 1870 with the Franco-Prussian War.

4. Peace has been the exception throughout the Old World.

5. America's Founders advised Americans to trade with the Old World but to have as little political connection with the Old World as possible because the Old World has complicated alliances and their principles of government are foreign to us.

6. An isolationist believes in no connections with a foreign country. A non-interventionist believes in trading with a foreign country and visiting a foreign country, but remaining neutral towards a foreign country's political affairs and refraining from forming alliances with other countries.

Chapter 13: Franco-Prussian War

Define

1. Alliances. When two or more governments stand together against a common enemy and for a common cause.

2. Reparations. Money, land, or goods forced from a defeated nation as compensation for damage or injury during a war.

Short Answer/Fill-In/True or False

3. Alliances are formed when two or more governments stand together against a common enemy and for a common cause. Shifting alliances happen when the governments quarrel, divorce, and form new partnerships, often with their former enemies, against their former friends. Shifting alliances sow the seeds for subsequent wars.

4. The German Empire was proclaimed on January 18, 1871, following the Franco-Prussian war.

Discussion/Essay/Assignment

5. Answers will vary.

Chapter 14: Ancient German Ambitions

Short Answer/Fill-In/True or False

1. Germany became a country in 1871.

2. Prussia originated in Lithuania more than a thousand years ago.

3. Prussia extended to the Rhine River in 1814.

4. Hitler's own generals first attempted to kill Adolph Hitler.

5. The **French** and **Austro-Hungarians** were the source of most of the worst warfare since the Middle Ages.

6. Answers will vary based on student's current knowledge and/or opinions. Save the answers. Students will be asked to revisit their answers.

Chapter 15: Political Power

Short Answer/Fill-In/True or False

1. Political power is the **legal privilege** of using force on persons who have not harmed anyone.

2. According to Uncle Eric, government is the institution that has the legal privilege of using force on persons who have not harmed anyone.

3. According to Uncle Eric, the legal privilege of using force on persons who have not harmed anyone is what sets government apart from all other institutions.

Discussion/Essay/Assignment

4. Answers will vary.

5. Answers will vary.

6. Answers will vary.

7. Answers will vary.

8. Answers will vary.

Chapter 16: Global Protection

Define

1. Global protection. The belief that a government has the right and duty to use its soldiers, sailors, and airmen to protect its citizens anywhere they choose to go, no matter how much risk they choose to take.

Short Answer/Fill-In/True or False

2. The idea of global protection for Americans began during the Barbary Wars.

For Discussion

3. Answers will vary.

4. Answers will vary.

Chapter 17: Interests

Define

1. Interests are undefined in law or the Constitution. They are often cited as a reason for the government to get into a war—to protect its interests.

2. Gunboat diplomacy. Using military force to frighten foreigners into signing agreements.

Short Answer/Fill-In/True or False

3. By the year **1855** the idea that the U.S. armed forces were strictly for defense of our homeland was gone.

Discussion/Essay/Assignment

4. Letters will vary.

5. Answers will vary.

Chapter 18: Cost Externalization

Define

1. Cost externalization. Shifting costs onto someone who does not get the benefits. Usually done covertly.

Short Answer/Fill-In/True or False

2. Answers will vary. Examples might include, but are not limited to: Watts riots; school integration in the South; protection of people and property following hurricanes or floods; National Guard in airports after September 11, 2001 World Trade Center attacks.

3. When an individual or firm goes abroad they go at their own risk; if they do not like the risk, they should not go.

4. No, the U.S. does not strictly practice this policy. Examples: Sierra Leone in 1997, United Fruit Company in Latin America.

5. In the Middle Ages, if threats to a business were so great that the necessary fortifications to protect it would be highly expensive, the investment in the business would not be made and workers would not be sent. The risks would not be taken.

6. Americans send their ships, their money, or themselves abroad, then when they become trapped in a war, they ask their U.S. government to send America's armed forces to help rescue them.

For Research

7. Research will vary.

Chapter 19: Manifest Destiny

Define

1. Mamelukes. A military group originally composed of slaves from Turkey. They ruled Egypt from about 1250 until 1517, and remained powerful there until 1811.

2. Manifest Destiny. The belief that God gave the U.S. government the right to capture and rule all the land from the Atlantic to the Pacific.

3. Imperialist. One who wishes to conquer others and force them into his empire.

Discussion/Essay/Assignment

4. Answers will vary.

Chapter 20: The Splendid Little War

Discussion/Essay/Assignment

1. Answers will vary.

2. Answers will vary.

Chapter 21: Guerrilla War

Define

1. Battalion. In the infantry, about 800 troops. Typically, but not always, there are nine troops in a squad, three squads to a platoon, four platoons to a company, six companies to a battalion, two battalions to a brigade, and six brigades to a division.

Short Answer/Fill-In/True or False

2. True. Most wars today are guerrilla wars.

3. True. Uncle Eric says that the events that led to World War I are more important than events during the war.

4. Switzerland has the best track record for staying out of wars.

5. Regulars are sometimes called conventional troops.

6. Militia are so-called citizen-soldiers like those required by the Second Amendment to the U.S. Constitution.

7. According to the AMERICAN HERITAGE DICTIONARY, a guerrilla is "a member of an irregular, usually indigenous military or paramilitary unit operating in small bands in occupied territory to harass and undermine the enemy, as by surprise raids."

8. Key points about guerrilla fighters are:

    a. A guerrilla usually will not attack unless he is sure he can escape cleanly.

    b. A guerrilla's style is hit-and-run.

    c. A guerrilla becomes a regular citizen during the day. A guerrilla can be a farmer, merchant, or taxi driver by day, and a sniper or saboteur by night. They are not easily found. They don't wear uniforms.

9. Among military experts, conventional troops need at least a six-to-one numerical superiority over guerrillas. If guerrillas number 1,000, the regulars fighting them will need to number at least 6,000.

Discussion/Essay/Assignment

10. The Second Amendment is in the Constitution because when a militia is well-armed and trained to fight an invader by using guerrilla tactics, an invader needs a force so large that no one is likely to try attempt it.

11. Answers will vary.

For Further Reading

12. Sources for reading selection will vary.

Chapter 22: Guerrilla War Examples

Short Answer/Fill-In/True or False

1. Militia-guerrillas are trained to target officers. Without leaders and strategists, the regular troops have no orders or strategy to follow.

2. A militia is defensive.

3. The point of the William Tell story is that the military objective is not to kill the enemy's troops. It is to kill enemy leaders.

4. The American armed forces are offensive.

Discussion/Essay/Assignment

5. Answers will vary.

6. Essays will vary.

7. Interpretations will vary.

8. Answers will vary.

For Further Reading

9. Student should read FEDERALIST PAPERS #20, #42 and #43.

Chapter 23: Never Surrender

Short Answer/Fill-In/True or False

1. Characteristics of guerrillas are:
   a. They are independent.
   b. They have no commander-in-chief.
   c. They have no central leader.
   d. They almost always operate on their own personal initiative.
   e. They are usually defensive.
   f. They are usually part-time soldiers.

2. A central authority is a convenience to the enemy because it gives the enemy the ability to force surrender onto the whole country just by conquering its government.

Discussion/Essay/Assignment

3. Answers will vary.

Chapter 24: Killing Women

Short Answer/Fill-In/True or False

1. A consequence on the regular troops of fighting a guerrilla war is that they are unable to recognize the enemy, so facing continued casualties they can lose control and commit murder and mayhem on any and all suspected guerrillas or anyone who is suspected of helping guerrillas. Morale drops. Desertion increases. Exhaustion increases.

2. Possessing modern weapons can tip the scale in favor of a guerrilla fighter.

3. The U.S. conquest of **the Philippines** was a crucial step toward the World Wars.

Chapter 25: Take No Prisoners

Define

1. Take No Prisoners. Kill everyone, even those who try to surrender.

Short Answer/Fill-In/True or False

2. According to Uncle Eric, the U.S. government now had the beginnings of its global empire and was solidly entrenched as a power that would not hesitate to stop anyone who got in its way.

Chapter 26: The White Man's Burden and the Ugly American

Define

1. White Man's Burden. The belief that the U.S. government and British government have the right to conquer other nations, especially dark-skinned non-Christians.

2. Anglo-Saxonism. White Man's Burden. The term Anglo-Saxon generally refers to English speaking whites of British cultural descent.

3. Barbarian. A person with a civilization regarded as primitive. A hazy term, barbarian was originally an ancient Roman word for northern Europeans who were not Roman.

Short Answer/Fill-In/True or False

4. Washington's burden is a synonym for the White Man's Burden.

5. In 2001, the U.S. government was thrown off the United Nation's Human Rights Committee and replaced by the government of Sudan. U.S. officials were told that they were being taught a lesson, not only by their enemies, but also by their allies in Europe who were giving notice that the U.S. government had become too arrogant.

For Further Reading

6. Kipling said that going to war against these darker-skinned people was difficult and dangerous but it had to be done in order to bring these people to a better way of life. The white man had to put an end to "sloth and heathen folly."

To View or For Further Reading

7. The "Ugly American" referred to the belief that America is superior to the rest of the world and has the right to force its ways onto others.

Chapter 27: The Great White Fleet

Short Answer/Fill-In/True or False

1. Theodore Roosevelt sent his Great White Fleet of 16 new battleships around the world to demonstrate that Washington was now a global power.

2. By the 1890s, America was the undisputed industrial leader of the world.

3. From the time of the Great White Fleet on, it was clear to every other government in the world that when they got into a war it would be a great advantage to get the U.S. involved in it on their side.

4. Uncle Eric believes that the Spanish-American War and conquest of the Philippines were the most important conflicts the U.S. has ever fought because it was during these conflicts that Americans stopped thinking like the 1776 Sons of Liberty and began thinking like the enemy that the 1776 Sons of Liberty were fighting—the Europeans.

Discussion/Essay/Assignment

5. Answers will vary.

Chapter 28: Up Close and Personal

Define

1. Area bombing. A British term from World War II. The bombing of civilian housing areas for the purpose of killing and terrorizing civilian men, women, and children, done mostly by the British to Germans, but also done to some extent by Americans to Germans, and to a greater extent by Americans to Japanese.

2. Delayed stress syndrome. An emotional illness caused by the stress of combat. In World War I, called shell shock. In World War II, battle fatigue.

3. Fragging. Tossing a fragmentation grenade into an officer's tent by one of his own men. Also used more generally to refer to any means of killing a higher-ranking person.

Short Answer/Fill-In/True or False

4. Answers will vary.

Chapter 29: The First Casualty of War

Define

1. War fever. An intense desire for war.

Discussion/Essay/Assignment

2. Answers will vary.

3. Lists will vary.

4. Answers will vary.

Chapter 30: Stealing Panama

Short Answer/Fill-In/True or False

1. After the Spanish-American War and conquest of the Philippines, the practice of using American military personnel for reasons other than the defense of America was solidly entrenched—and it remains so.

2. The U.S. government wanted Panama so Teddy Roosevelt sent U.S. marines to help the Panamanians successfully rebel against Colombian forces. The Panamanians won, set up an independent government, and allowed Washington to build the Panama Canal. This reinforced the notion that American troops should be used for purposes other than defense of America.

Chapter 31: Helping Crooks and Tyrants

Define

1. Fungible. Each unit is indistinguishable from another, so each can substitute for another. Money is fungible. This means one dollar can substitute for any other dollar.

Short Answer/Fill-In/True or False

2. The Constitution and Bill of Rights protect people inside the borders of the United States. They offer no protection to anyone outside U.S. borders. Outside the U.S. there are few limits to the U.S. government's use of power.

Discussion/Essay/Assignment

3. Student should select from one of the persons listed and research that individual.

4. Answers will vary.

5. If you help one government nonmilitarily, the monies received frees up that government's money for additional arms purchases, oftentimes used against its own people, as well as its enemies.

6. George Washington cautioned Americans against "attachments" with other nations because an attachment (alliance) to one nation can cause hatred from the enemies of that nation towards those in alliance. All governments have enemies. If the U.S. government helps one government, their enemies become our enemies. This is part of the legacy of the events that led up to World War I. It is what George Washington cautioned about in his Farewell Address. Uncle Eric says that the U.S. support for the Egyptian dictatorship is one of the reasons behind the September 11 attacks.

For Research

7. Research exercise. Students' conclusions may vary based on the data found.

For Further Reading

8. Read Dr. Seuss' anti-fascist story YERTLE THE TURTLE.

Chapter 32: The Usual Suspects

Short Answer/Fill-In/True or False

1. In alphabetical order, the Usual Suspects are: Beijing, Berlin, London, Moscow, Paris, Rome, Tokyo, Vienna, and Washington.

2. To be on the list of Usual Suspects a government has to completely embrace the Deadly Ideas that lead to war.

For Research

3. Answers will vary based on research.

Chapter 33: Boxer Rebellion and Russo-Japanese War

Define

1. Yihequan. A Chinese guerrilla group that fought the Boxer Rebellion against foreign powers. The word "yihequan" means righteous and harmonious fists.

Short Answer/Fill-In/True or False

2. In 1898, the Chinese rebelled against foreign rule. Militia units called Yihequan, which means "righteous and harmonious fists", spearheaded the rebellion. The name led to the foreign press calling the rebels the Boxers.

3. The Russo-Japanese War was the first conflict in modern times in which an Asian power defeated a European power (the Mongols had done it during the Middle Ages). This war can be seen as the beginning of the Japanese attempt to copy what the U.S. had done in the Spanish-American War—that is, to start building its own empire by stealing territory from the people who had stolen it first, the Europeans.

For Research

4. Answers will vary based on research.

Chapter 34: Choosing Up Sides

Short Answer/Fill-In/True or False

1. Prussia's Count Otto von Bismark said, "A generation that has taken a beating is always followed by a generation that deals one".

2. The Austro-Hungarians and the Germans formed an alliance that became the cornerstone of what would eventually become the Central Powers in World War I.

3. Italy, Germany, and Austria-Hungary formed the so-called Triple Alliance in World War I.

4. Italy, Germany, and Austria-Hungary formed the core of the Central Powers in World War I.

5. Italy, Germany, and Austria-Hungary formed the core of the Axis in World War II.

6. Italy switched sides in both World Wars.

7. Britain, France, and Russia formed the core of the Allies in World War I.

8. Britain, France, and Russia formed the core of the Allies in World War II.

For Research

9. Research answers will vary.

To View

10. Watch the film: THE ADVENTURES OF YOUNG INDIANA JONES: DEMONS OF DECEPTION.

Chapter 35: The Morocco Crisis

Short Answer/Fill-In/True or False

1. The two deadly ideas that led to the Morocco crisis are:
   a. Global protection: The German government sent the gunboat *Panther* to protect Germans in Morocco during the Moroccan revolution of 1911.
   b. Interests: The French saw the *Panther* as a threat to French control of Morocco.

2. To keep the Germans and French from going to war, the French government gave the German government land in Black equatorial Africa.

3. No, the Africans were not asked if it was okay with them to be ruled by Germans. This carving up of the world by governments without the consent of the peoples involved is one reason for the long-standing hatreds among peoples living on those lands.

Chapter 36: Alliances

Short Answer/Fill-In/True or False

1. One of the most important lessons to learn from World War I is that alliances turn small wars into big ones.

2. The killing of one man, Archduke Ferdinand, created a chain reaction that turned that event into World War I because of the promises countries made to each other to come to each other's defense—alliances, the ninth deadly idea that leads to war.

3. Switzerland, for two centuries, had remained neutral, avoiding military alliances.

4. According to Uncle Eric, the U.S. government formed new alliances after World War II, some with the governments of Israel, Saudi Arabia, Egypt, and other powers in the Mideast. These alliances led to the September 11th attacks and the war that followed.

Chapter 37: The Glory of War

Define

1. Trench sweeper. A small, portable machine gun.

2. The Great War. The original name for the First World War. The term was abandoned after the Second World War.

Short Answer/Fill-In/True or False

3. The machine gun changed the face of war and helped create conditions that led to the Treaty of Versailles, which led to World War II.

Discussion/Essay/Assignment

4. Answers will vary.

For Research

5. From WEBSTER'S NEW WORLD DICTIONARY OF THE AMERICAN LANGUAGE, COLLEGE EDITION, published by The World Publishing Company, copyright 1962, examples of diseases that resulted from trench warfare include: trench fever, trench foot, trench mouth.

6. Examples of the type of weaponry introduced in World War I include: flame throwers, machine gun, mustard gas.

Chapter 38: America's Entry Into World War I

Short Answer/Fill-In/True or False

1. In 1914 Germany was **43** years old.
2. On January 18, 1871, the German Empire was proclaimed.
3. Germany built its new empire by stealing land and taxpayers from the governments who had conquered and stolen ahead of them.
4. Britain, France, and Russia regarded Germany as an aggressor.
5. As the "mother countries" entered wars, they dragged their colonies in with them.
6. The battle line between France and Germany moved little more than three miles during the entire course of World War I.
7. True. When World War I erupted, President Wilson had declared that the U.S. would remain neutral.
8. Global protection was the deadly idea that leads to war that was exemplified by the sinking of the *Lusitania.* President Wilson pledged to protect Americans no matter how risky the waters in which they chose to sail.
9. According to Uncle Eric, U.S. President Woodrow Wilson saved the war by declaring war against Germany on April 6, 1917.
10. The entry of the U.S. into the war caused World War I to become the first global war.

Discussion/Essay/Assignment

11. Answers will vary.

For Research

12. Research results will vary.

Chapter 39: The Third Choice Ignored

Short Answer/Fill-In/True or False

1. Germany surrendered on November 11, 1918.

Discussion/Essay/Assignment

2. Essays will vary.

3. Answers will vary.

4. Answers will vary.

5. For discussion.

6. Essays will vary.

For Further Reading

7. Read EXTRAORDINARY POPULAR DELUSIONS AND THE MADNESS OF CROWDS by Charles Mackay.

Chapter 40: They Will Fight Over Anything

Short Answer/Fill-In/True or False

1. The wars of Europe and Asia became World Wars when the U.S. got involved in them.

Chapter 41: The Treaty of Versailles

Define

1. *Lebensraum.* German for living space. The reason Hitler launched his attack on the U.S.S.R. was to capture land for Germans to expand into.

Short Answer/Fill-In/True or False

2. The good guys in World War I were the Allies.

3. True. The Allied rulers blamed the First World War on the German government as well as the German people.

4. Keynes quit the conference because he believed the terms of the Treaty of Versailles would so impoverish the Germans that it would lead to another great war.

5. Hitler invaded Poland 20 years after the Treaty of Versailles.

6. The essential chain of events in World War I that led to World War II are:

    a. Washington entered the war under the deadly idea of global protection.

    b. America's fresh troops and weapons tipped the scale in favor of the Allies.

    c. The Allies forced the Treaty of Versailles onto the German government and the German people.

    d. The Treaty forced the German people to pay for the damages of the war, making the German people destitute and desperate.

Discussion/Essay/Assignment

7. Answers will vary.

Chapter 42: The Sound of Reloading

Short Answer/Fill-In/True or False

1. The Treaty of Versailles marked the end of World War I and the beginning of World War II.

2. The Germans began to rearm when the British and French refused to disarm, thus breaking the disarmament agreement, freeing Germany from its contractual obligations.

Chapter 43: Hitler's Rise

Define

1. League of Nations. Predecessor of the United Nations; the first attempt to create a world government. The failure of the League of Nations to stop Italy's invasion of Ethiopia is often cited as a cause of World War II. Many Americans bemoan the loss of the League and the incompetence of the United Nations because they believe a single world government that can force its will onto anyone, anywhere, is the way to create peace and liberty for all.

2. Nationalism. Intense devotion to one's nation; intense patriotism.

3. Aryan race. A Nazi propaganda term meaning a Nordic Caucasian of non-Jewish descent.

Short Answer/Fill-In/True or False

4. Hitler got his start during the German hyperinflation.

5. The German government printed money to pay its penalties.

6. The German people blamed the Allies for their deprivation.

7. In July, 1921, Adolph Hitler became leader of the Nazi Party.

8. Nazism is a form of fascism.

9. In 1923 the Nazi Party tried to take over the government of the German state of Bavaria. Hitler went to prison.

10. While in prison, Hitler wrote MEIN KAMPF.

11. MEIN KAMPF explains Hitler's ideas on anti-Semitism, anti-Communism, superiority of the so-called Aryan race, German nationalism, and the state's superiority over the individual. Mein kampf means "My Battle" and is the handbook of Nazism.

12. The U.S. government expanded the U.S. money supply, sending much of the new money to Germany.

13. Much of the newly created money went into the U.S. stock market creating a huge speculative bubble.

14. The Federal Reserve stopped expanding the money supply, the stock bubble burst, and the Great Depression began.

15. No, the depression was world-wide.

16. Germany was hit hardest by the depression.

For Further Reading

17. Read the chapter titled "Capitalism and Other Isms" in Karl Hess' book CAPITALISM FOR KIDS.

Chapter 44: U.S. Invades Russia

Define

1. Cossacks. An ethnic group located mostly in southern Russia. Militantly Christian, Cossacks were "the sword arm of the Czars" against the Turks (Muslims), and against anyone who rebelled against the Czars.

Short Answer/Fill-In/True or False

2. The U.S. invaded Russia in **1918**.

3. The U.S. invaded Russia under the deadly idea of protecting "interests."

4. The Cold War began in 1945.

5. Russia did not trust the U.S. because of the U.S. invasion of Russia in 1918.

Discussion/Essay/Assignment

6. The U.S. invaded Russia in 1918 under the deadly idea of "interests" to conquer the Bolsheviks, who were socialists.

For Research

7. Answers may vary based on who is in power at the time the research is conducted.

To View

8. DOCTOR ZHIVAGO starring Omar Sharif and Julie Christie.

Chapter 45: Desperation and the Neutrality Act

Define

1. Conscription. Compulsory enrollment in the armed services.

Short Answer/Fill-In/True or False

2. Hitler became popular in Germany because he gave the German people hope that their poverty and suffering would end.

3. The Nazi Party took control of the German government in March 1933.

4. The first concentration camp was erected at Dachau in March 1933.

5. Hitler proclaimed himself Fuhrer in August 1934.

6. A command economy is one in which government agencies order businesses and individuals to do whatever the agencies believed necessary. Under these orders, German businesses hired workers and unemployment fell.

7. German businesses and workers were producing weapons.

8. Hitler introduced conscription in 1935.

9. The Neutrality Act required that the U.S. stay out of the Old World's wars, and that the U.S. offer no assistance to governments in these wars. Congress also ordered the President to give no protection to U.S. citizens who take the risk of entering a war zone.

10. Uncle Eric says he knows of no greater mistake in morals and judgment than Washington's participation in World War I and the resulting Treaty of Versailles, which led to World War II.

For Further Reading

11. Read the chapter titled "Wallpaper, Wheelbarrows and Recessions" from the book WHATEVER HAPPENED TO PENNY CANDY? by Richard J. Maybury.

Chapter 46: Summary

Short Answer/Fill-In/True or False

1. True. A fundamental belief of America's Founders was that political power corrupts the morals and the judgment.

2. False. The correct statement is: According to America's Founders, the power and size of the U.S. government should be kept as limited as possible.

3. False. The correct statement is: In foreign affairs, George Washington believed that the U.S. government must be neutral.

4. It was the **United States** government's participation in the garden-variety European and Asian wars that turned them into World Wars.

5. The ten deadly ideas that lead to war are: Pax Romana, fascism, love of political power, global protection, interests, cost externalization, Manifest Destiny, alliances, the glory of war, and the White Man's Burden (now Washington's Burden).

6. The Second Amendment to the U.S. Constitution provides for a **well-regulated militia**.

Discussion/Essay/Assignment

7. Essays will vary.

8. Answers will vary.

Thought Exercises Revisited

1. Answers will vary.

2. Answers will vary.

3. Answers will vary.

Final Exam Answers

1. Patriotism. Dedication to the principles on which the country was founded, and a willingness to stand firm and fight for these principles regardless of what the government says or does.

2. The two laws that make civilization possible are: 1) Do all you have agreed to do, and 2) do not encroach on other persons or their property.

3. America's Founders believed that political power corrupts the morals and the judgment and that no one can be trusted with it, so government must be kept very limited.

4. The **Italian** government switched sides in World War I, starting the war on the side of the Central Powers and ending on the side of the Allies.

5. According to Uncle Eric, the cause of World War II is World War I.

6. Propaganda. Strongly biased information designed to persuade, usually relating to political or economic matters. The bias is often subtle and usually hidden and may make use of lies and half-truths.

7. Foreign policy. The government's behavior toward other governments and toward persons in other lands.

8. False. The correct answer is: Taking territory makes an army weaker because as an army advances it must leave troops behind to occupy the conquered areas. This reduces the number of troops that are left to fight at the front lines. If this continually happens, the army continues to weaken at the front lines, and it will start losing.

9. Axis. In World War II, the alliance led by Berlin, Rome, and Tokyo. Enemies of the Allies.

10. Allies. In World War I, the alliance led by London, Moscow, and Washington. Enemies of the Central Powers. In World War II, the same group; enemies of the Axis.

11. Central Powers. In World War I, the group led by Germany and Austria-Hungary. Consisted of Germany, the Austro-Hungarian Empire, Turkey, and Bulgaria. Enemies of the Allies.

12. Fascism. The political philosophy that is no philosophy at all. Do whatever appears necessary. It is derived from the law of the Roman Empire.

13. For about nine centuries, the two dominant powers in Europe were the French Empire and the Austro-Hungarian Empire. The Austro-Hungarian Empire included the Holy Roman Empire and the Habsburg Empire.

14. True. According to Uncle Eric, fascism was regarded as a respectable philosophy until World War II.

15. Neutrality. Not aligned with, supporting, or favoring any side in a war or dispute.

16. Most historians say that the World Wars began in **1870** with the **Franco-Prussian War**.

17. An isolationist believes in no connections with a foreign country. A non-interventionist believes in trading with a foreign country and visiting a foreign country, but remaining neutral towards a foreign country's political affairs and refraining from forming alliances with other countries.

18. Alliances. When two or more governments stand together against a common enemy and for a common cause.

19. Reparations. Money, land, or goods forced from a defeated nation as compensation for damage or injury during a war.

20. The **German** Empire was proclaimed on January 18, 1871, following the Franco-Prussian war.

21. The **French** and **Austro-Hungarians** were the source of most of the worst warfare since the Middle Ages.

22. Political power. The legal privilege of using force on persons who have not harmed anyone.

23. Global protection. The belief that a government has the right and duty to use its soldiers, sailors, and airmen to protect its citizens anywhere they choose to go, no matter how much risk they choose to take.

24. The idea of global protection for Americans began during the **Barbary** Wars.

25. By the year **1855** the idea that the U.S. armed forces were strictly for defense of our homeland was gone.

26. Cost externalization. Shifting costs onto someone who does not get the benefits. Usually done covertly.

27. True. Most wars today are guerrilla wars.

28. **Switzerland** is the nation that has the best track record for staying out of wars.

29. Three key points about guerrilla fighters are:

    a. A guerrilla usually will not attack unless he is sure he can escape cleanly.

    b. A guerrilla's style is hit-and-run.

    c. A guerrilla becomes a regular citizen during the day. A guerrilla can be a farmer, merchant, or taxi driver by day, and a sniper or saboteur by night. They are not easily found. They don't wear uniforms.

30. Militia-guerrillas are trained to target officers. Without leaders and strategists, the regular troops have no orders or strategy to follow.

31. A militia is defensive.

32. The American armed forces are offensive.

33. A central authority is a convenience to the enemy because it gives the enemy the ability to force surrender onto the whole country just by conquering its government.

34. By the 1890s, America was the undisputed industrial leader of the world.

35. After the Spanish-American War and conquest of the Philippines, the practice of using American military personnel for reasons other than the defense of America was solidly entrenched—and it remains so.

36. In alphabetical order, the Usual Suspects are: Beijing, Berlin, London, Moscow, Paris, Rome, Tokyo, Vienna, and Washington.

37. The Russo-Japanese War was the first conflict in modern times in which an Asian power defeated a European power (the Mongols had done it during the Middle Ages). This war can be seen as the beginning of the Japanese attempt to copy what the U.S. had done in the Spanish-American War—that is, to start building its own empire by stealing territory from the people who had stolen it first, the Europeans.

38. The **Austro-Hungarians** and the **Germans** formed an alliance that became the cornerstone of what would eventually become the Central Powers in World War I.

39. One of the most important lessons to learn from World War I is that **alliances** turn small wars into big ones.

40. The machine gun changed the face of war and helped create conditions that led to the Treaty of Versailles, which led to World War II.

41. The battle line between France and Germany moved little more than three miles during the entire course of World War I.

42. True. When World War I erupted, President Wilson had declared that the U.S. would remain neutral.

43. The entry of the U.S. into the war caused World War I to become the first global war.

44. Germany surrendered on November 11, 1918.

45. True. The Allied rulers blamed the First World War on the German government as well as the German people.

46. According to Uncle Eric, the four essential chain of events in World War I that led to World War II are:

    a. Washington entered the war under the deadly idea of global protection.

    b. America's fresh troops and weapons tipped the scale in favor of the Allies.

    c. The Allies forced the Treaty of Versailles onto the German government and the German people.

    d. The Treaty forced the German people to pay for the damages of the war, making the German people destitute and desperate.

47. The Treaty of Versailles marked the end of World War I and the beginning of World War II.

48. The Germans began to rearm when the British and French refused to disarm, thus breaking the disarmament agreement, freeing Germany from its contractual obligations.

49. The Nazi Party took control of the German government in March 1933.

50. The ten deadly ideas that lead to war are: Pax Romana, fascism, love of political power, global protection, interests, cost externalization, Manifest Destiny, alliances, the glory of war, and the White Man's Burden (now Washington's Burden).

Essay: Quote selections and essays will vary.

Essay: Quote selections and essays will vary.

Quotes About War

"Injustice, arrogance, displayed in the hour of triumph will never be forgotten or forgiven."

David Lloyd George
Memo from the
World War I surrender conference, 1919

"Against war it may be said that it makes the victor stupid and the vanquished revengeful."

Friedrich Nietzsche
HUMAN, ALL TOO HUMAN, 1878

"If they want peace, nations should avoid the pinpricks that precede cannon shots."

Napoleon Bonaparte
Reported conversation with
Czar Alexander, 1807

"War involves in its progress such a train of unforeseen and unsupposed circumstances that no human wisdom can calculate the end. It has but one thing certain, and that is to increase taxes."

Thomas Paine
PROSPECTS ON THE RUBICON, 1787

"Nay, number itself in armies importeth not much, where the people is of weak courage; for as Virgil saith, 'It never troubles the wolf how many the sheep be.'"

Sir Francis Bacon
"Of The True Greatness of
Kingdoms and Estates"
ESSAYS, 1625

"I find war detestable but those who praise it without participating in it even more so."

Romain Rolland
"Inter arma caritas"
JOURNAL DE GENEVE, 1914

"They may ring their bells now, before long they will be wringing their hands."

Sir Robert Walpole
Speech about the celebrations in England
at the beginning of a war with Spain, 1739

"They make a desert and call it peace."

Tacitus
AGRICOLA, circa 98 A.D.

"All wars are wars among thieves who are too cowardly to fight and who therefore induce the young manhood of the whole world to do the fighting for them."

Emma Goldman
"Address to the Jury"
MOTHER EARTH, 1917

"There is many a boy here today who looks on war as all glory, but, boys, it is all hell."

William Tecumseh Sherman
Speech in Columbus, Ohio, 1880

"It is not merely cruelty that leads men to love war, it is excitement."

Henry Ward Beecher
PROVERBS FROM PLYMOUTH PULPIT, 1887

"As long as war is regarded as wicked, it will always have its fascination. When it is looked upon as vulgar, it will cease to be popular."

Oscar Wilde
INTENTIONS, 1891

"Once blood is shed in a national quarrel, reason and right are swept aside by the rage of angry men."

David Lloyd George
1933-36

"I tell you there's nothing to stop war from going on forever. ... A slight case of negligence, and it's bogged down up to the axles. And then it's a matter of hauling the war out of the mud again. But emperors and kings and popes will come to its rescue."

Bertolt Brecht
MOTHER COURAGE, 1939

"Diplomats are just as essential to starting a war as soldiers are for finishing it. You take diplomacy out of war and the thing would fall flat in a week."

Will Rogers
AUTOBIOGRAPHY OF WILL ROGERS, 1949

"We Smiths want peace so bad we are willing to kill every one of the Joneses to get it."

I.F. Stone
quoted in the TRUMAN ERA, 1949

"War is both the product of an earlier corruption and a producer of new corruptions."

Lewis Mumford
THE CONDUCT OF LIFE, 1951

"Every gun that is fired, every warship launched, every rocket fired signifies, in the final sense, a theft from those who hunger and are not fed, those who are cold and are not clothed. The world in arms is not spending money alone. It is spending the sweat of its laborers, the genius of its scientists, the hopes of its children."

President Dwight D. Eisenhower
Speech, 1953

"Past experience provides little basis for confidence that reason can prevail in an atmosphere of war fever."

J. William Fulbright
Speech to U.S. Senate, 1966

"There's nothing like a good war to make people feel important."

Congressional aide quoted in NEWSWEEK
October 10, 1990

"Laws are silent in time of war."

Cicero
PRO MILONE, 52 B.C.

"A general and a bit of shooting makes you forget your troubles ... it takes your mind off the cost of living."

Brendan Behan
THE HOSTAGE, 1958

"I believe that the real reason why war exists is because men have always liked war, and women, warriors."

Martin van Creveld
RISE AND DECLINE OF THE STATE, 1999

"Men love war because it allows them to look serious. Because it is the one thing that stops women laughing at them."

John Fowles
THE MAGUS, 1965

"The word state is identical with the word war."

Prince Peter Kropotkin
PAROLES D'UN REVOLTE, 1885

"We are not about to send American boys nine or ten thousand miles away from home to do what Asian boys ought to be doing for themselves."

President Lyndon B. Johnson
Speech about the Vietnam War, 1964

"In times of peace the people look most to their representatives; but in war, to the executive solely."

Thomas Jefferson
Letter to Caesar A. Rodney, 1810

"Everyone, when there's a war in the air, learns to live in a new element: falsehood."

Jean Giraudoux
TIGER AT THE GATES, 1935

"The Bill of Rights stops at the border."

Richard Maybury
WORLD WAR I: THE REST OF THE STORY, 2003

Suggested Viewing

(compiled by Richard Maybury and Jane Williams)

Parental discretion on all films (even when rated PG) due to sensitivities some students may have to the battle scenes.

ACES HIGH (1977) starring Christopher Plummer. Antiwar film focusing on the indoctrination of World War I pilots. Rated PG.

ALL QUIET ON THE WESTERN FRONT (1930). Good example of trench warfare. Excellent story of German soldiers in WWI who were encouraged to fight for the Fatherland and experience the glory of war.

ADVENTURES OF YOUNG INDIANA JONES, ATTACK OF THE HAWKMEN
ADVENTURES OF YOUNG INDIANA JONES, TRENCHES OF HELL (Somme 1916, Germany 1916)
ADVENTURES OF YOUNG INDIANA JONES, DEMONS OF DECEPTION (Verdun 1916, Paris 1916)

THE AFRICAN QUEEN (1951) starring Humphrey Bogart and Katharine Hepburn who travel down river in Africa during World War I combating the Germans and each other.

BREAKER MORANT (1979) starring Edward Woodward. Based on a true story. A superbly accurate picture of the British government's use of ethnic cleansing to build the British Empire under the doctrine of Anglo-Saxonism. Also shows how troops and governments are corrupted by anti-guerrilla warfare. Rated PG.

THE COLOR OF WAR. The segment called "Why We Fight" by the History Channel. Revealing look at the thinking of American soldiers, sailors, and airmen in World War II. Among other things, the film explains that in 1942 millions of Americans had no dislike of Germans and many admired them. The government had to use extreme propaganda against Germans so that these millions would hate them. This extreme message still colors our view of both World Wars.

THE DAWN PATROL (1938) starring Errol Flynn and Basil Rathbone. World War I film about officer who must send inexperienced pilots into combat.

GALLIPOLI (1981). A portion of the film shows the disastrous Gallipoli campaign in Turkey during World War I. Perhaps more revealing, however, is the shallow thinking and strong emotions that lead young men (and now women) to march off to war. Rated PG.

GETTYSBURG (1993) starring Tom Berenger. Shows how lines of men with rifles would rush at each other as they had been doing in Europe for centuries and did again in World War I. Rated PG.

LAWRENCE OF ARABIA (1962) starring Peter O'Toole and Alec Guiness. Assigned to Arabia during World War I, Lawrence unites the warring Arab factions into a strong guerrilla front where they eventually defeat the ruling Turkish Empire. Rated PG.

THE LIGHTHORSEMEN (1987) starring Simon Wincer and Anthony Andrews. Story of the Australian Light Horse Brigade and a World War I desert campaign. Rated PG.

ON THE FRONT LINES produced by Walt Disney Studios. On December 8, 1941, the Disney Studio was taken over by the military as part of the war effort. Walt Disney spent the next four years creating and producing training, propaganda, and educational films for the Armed Forces. Also included in this collection is the full-length feature propaganda film VICTORY THROUGH AIR POWER released in 1943.

THE PATRIOT starring Mel Gibson. Another depiction of young men with rifles rushing at each other. But more, shows the effectiveness of guerrilla warfare. Rated R. (Quite violent)

SANDS OF IWO JIMA (1949) starring John Wayne. Uses some authentic World War II combat footage. When Marine trainees in 1961 at Camp Pendleton were asked why they had enlisted, half said it was because they had been inspired by SANDS OF IWO JIMA.

SERGEANT YORK (1941) starring Gary Cooper. Story of pacifist Alvin York who lost four appeals after registering for the draft. He was assigned to a front-line rifle company during World War I. Excellent story.

THEY WERE EXPENDABLE (1945) starring John Wayne. This is a classic World War II propaganda film aimed at the hearts and minds of young men.

THE UGLY AMERICAN (1963) starring Marlon Brando as the American ambassador to an Asian country. Shows U.S. power struggle.

VICTORY AT SEA. The 1954 television series produced by Henry Salomon that gives the government's side of the story about World War II. If you do not have the time to watch all 26 segments, they have been compressed into a two-hour movie often shown on television.

WHY WE FIGHT directed by Frank Capra. In World War II, the federal government wanted a series of films that would explain why Americans should support the fight. The result was the series WHY WE FIGHT which was so persuasive that it became the unquestioned explanation of *both* World Wars. This film will give you a quick yet profound understanding of why Americans believe what they do about the World Wars. Highly recommended by Richard Maybury.

ZULU (1964) starring Michael Caine. British expansion into Africa in the 19th century provokes attack by the Zulu tribe against British occupation. This film recreated the 1879 battle where 105 men of the South Wales Borderers defended their outpost against 4000 Zulu warriors.

..."a passionate attachment of one nation for another produces a variety of evils. Sympathy for the favorite nation, facilitating the illusion of an imaginary common interest in cases where no real common interest exists, and infusing into one the enmities of the other, betrays the former into a participation in the quarrels and wars of the latter, without adequate inducement or justification. It leads also to concession to the favorite nation of privileges denied to others, which is apt doubly to injure the nation making the concessions; by unnecessarily parting with what ought to have been retained; and by exciting jealousy, ill-will and a disposition to retaliate, in the parties from whom equal privileges are withheld. And it gives to ambitious, corrupted or deluded citizens (who devote themselves to the favorite nation) facility to betray, or sacrifice the interests of their own country, without odium, sometimes even with popularity .... Against the insidious wiles of foreign influence, (I conjure you to believe me fellow-citizen) the jealousy of a free people ought to be constantly awake."

—George Washington
WASHINGTON'S FAREWELL ADDRESS, 1796

"Never was so much false arithmetic employed on any subject, as that which has been employed to persuade nations that it is in their interest to go to war."

—Thomas Jefferson, 1782

"I have ever deemed it fundamental for the United States never to take active part in the quarrels of Europe. Their political interests are entirely distinct from ours. Their mutual jealousies, their balance of power, their complicated alliances, their forms and principles of government, are all foreign to us. They are nations of eternal war."

—Thomas Jefferson, 1823